KINGDOMS IN CONFLICT

KINGDOMS IN CONFLICT

David Pawson

Anchor Recordings

First published in Great Britain in 2015 by
Anchor Recordings Ltd
72 The Street, Kennington, Ashford TN24 9HS

**For more of David Pawson's teaching,
including DVDs and CDs, go to
www.davidpawson.com**

**FOR FREE DOWNLOADS
www.davidpawson.org**

**For further information, email
info@davidpawsonministry.com**

ISBN 978-1-909886-04-9

Printed by Lightning Source

Contents

This book is based on a series of talks. Originating as it does from the spoken word, its style will be found by many readers to be somewhat different from my usual written style. It is hoped that this will not detract from the substance of the biblical teaching found here.

As always, I ask the reader to compare everything I say or write with what is written in the Bible and, if at any point a conflict is found, always to rely upon the clear teaching of scripture.

David Pawson

1

THE KINGDOM OF GOD

Please read: Psalm 2; Daniel 4:28–37 (a passage which always leaves me trembling); 1 Chronicles 29:10–end.

I believe that God is looking for men and women whose orientation is towards the kingdom rather than their parish or their little fellowship or their family or their immediate circumstances – people who have got a big enough mind and heart to seek first, before anything else, his kingdom where they live. I believe that is a big enough task for us to really prepare for. Anything less than that is less than God's goal.

People sometimes talk about a change of government, by which they mean a change of party or a change of policy or leader, or even a change of system. Jesus' message was that the basic need of this world is a change of government but he did not use that word, he used the word "kingdom".

I want to describe for you what it is like to live in a kingdom. So what kind of government is a kingdom? The answer is very simple and quite different from the kind of government we have in the UK. We British are masters at compromise, even muddle. We revel in calling ourselves a kingdom when we have not been a kingdom for centuries, because reigning is not the same as ruling. At the time of writing, Queen Elizabeth reigns but the Government of the day actually rules. That is not a kingdom (in the Bible's sense of the word). I often pity the Queen because she has to reign without ruling and has very little power indeed. Over the centuries we have steadily robbed our monarch of any chance of ruling. One of the few prerogatives the Queen still has is that if in a general election there were a dead heat she would have the casting vote! But I can hardly imagine that ever happening, can you? In fact, I saw a list of the only things that the Queen can do by way of exercising her own authority. There were only ten things on that list and most of them were emergency acts. In other countries there may be an elected President and we retain an inherited "presidency" but in fact it is still republican rather than royal in its outworking. My point is that *we do not really know what it is like to live in a kingdom* even if we think we do. I have never yet had to make any decision in daily life which required me to pay attention to what the Queen wished. Have you? Can you think of any moment in your life when you stopped and said, "Now what would the Queen want me to do in this situation?" We just don't even take her will into account. We may like to see her parade and we may cheer her and wave union flags, but we have no intention of letting her rule over us.

There was a big debate between King James VI of Scotland and George Buchanan his tutor, who tried to teach the future king that he derived his sovereignty from the people and that he must always defer to the will of the people, and that they had a perfect right to get rid of him if he didn't. Because the future King James loathed his tutor intensely, he read secretly some books by a French philosopher who wrote: "Kings should rule as well as reign; in a kingdom the king's wish is law" – and James, who would also become James I of England, tried to return to a true kingdom, in reaction to his tutor. It was that – and his passing on that view to King Charles I – which led ultimately to the latter's execution.

I can now tell you what a kingdom is. It is a people ruled by one man, and that one man's will is law. He has no government to debate his will, he simply declares his will.

He has that job of reigning and ruling by inheritance. He is king because he was the son of a father who was also king. He has no cabinet and certainly there is no opposition. He is not put into that position by a vote nor can he be voted out of that position. That is a kingdom and so the UK is not really a kingdom.

Throughout the Bible, from cover to cover, the concept of kingship is that the king rules as well as reigns. I have a question to ask you (which I believe was from the Lord on an occasion when I taught on this, and I ask you to check it in your spirit before you accept it): "Why do you expect me to act as sovereign when you are not willing to be my subjects?"

It is one of the failings of human nature when it has not experienced a kingdom to desire sovereignty without becoming subject. In election campaigns I hear many people discussing what the next government should do for us, but I never hear a discussion of the responsibility of citizens towards the government – how we could get together and finance what we want the government to do. We tend to leave that to them. In the same way, as people who have been accustomed to this kind of thinking, Christians may allow the spirit of the world to creep into their thinking. It is part of our failing that we want God to act sovereignly in our land and we pray for him to do so but we do not discuss the other side of the kingdom, which is how to be subject to the rule of the King.

Let me explain what I mean: in the early days of the spiritual renewal (for which we all praise God) I sensed that there were many people who were seeking to have God's sovereignty exercised over them in the sense of healing their diseases, taking away their depressions, giving them answers to the problems for which they sought guidance – but there were very few asking the Spirit to tell them how to be subject to the kingly rule of Jesus Christ.

Announce a healing meeting and you could guarantee a large attendance. But our bodies are to be the temples of the Holy Spirit. That means God was looking not just for bodies to heal but for bodies he could rule. If your body is ruled by the King of heaven then that is an end to gluttony, an end to drunkenness, an end to sex outside marriage, and a whole lot of other things. There were thousands who wanted God to exercise sovereignty over their disease, but not so many who wanted God to exercise sovereignty over their bodies. My burden is this — because the kingdom of heaven belongs to those who are subject – those who are concerned with the kingdom will not just be praying for God to exercise his sovereignty, whether in healing or other release or in revival, but will be seeking to bring the nation into subjection to his will – and in subjection to him there is perfect freedom.

Every kingdom is made up of two parts. On the one hand it has a sovereign, but a kingdom is incomplete if it just has a sovereign. A kingdom is complete when the sovereign has subjects who willingly accept his leadership.

Let us rush straight through to another conclusion. One of the questions I get asked most frequently is: "Shall I stay in my church or not?" Have you at least considered that question? Do you want to know my answer to it? You are going to be disappointed. My answer is very simple: you obey the King—that is all. If the king tells you to move then you do so. If the king tells you to stay in, you stay in. That is your sole concern if you want to be a subject of the King. It seems to me that he is telling some people to stay in and some people to move. It is quite wrong for either group to tell the other what they should be doing. What we should be encouraging each other to do is obey the king, not to weigh up the pros and cons, not to consider the consequences, but to say, "Lord, you are King." God is looking for subjects, he is not just looking for those who will say, "God, will you act sovereignly in our land? Will you sweep through with revival? Will you take over? Will you smash this? Will you deal with that? Will you clear up disorder? Will you deal with violence?" How much we want God to act as sovereign! Yet he is looking for subjects.

It was the Lord's own problem, and later we shall look at the kingdom of heaven in the life of Jesus. I can sum up his problem in one sentence: the people wanted a sovereign but Jesus was looking for subjects and he could not find them—that was the crisis. They wanted a king who would release them, deliver them, feed them and look after them via a kind of mini welfare state, all in himself, but when he spelt out in detail in the Sermon on the Mount what it was to be a subject of the kingdom, as we shall see, he could not find anyone who was willing to be subject.

You may already be a true subject of the King. Do you hope that God would act sovereignly in some situation in your life, your family or in some health issue? Well, he may do, and I marvel at Jesus, that he was willing to cleanse lepers who did not even come back to say thank you. Nevertheless, I believe God is looking for subjects and then he can exercise his sovereignty here. It is not that he is helpless without subjects, but my burden is to combine sovereignty and subjection, though even the word "subjection" is anathema to us. We do not like to be considered as "subjects", subject to another's will. Now how would you like to live in a kingdom? Would you welcome it or not? My answer is that this would entirely depend on the King. If he was a good king, I would welcome it. If he was a bad king, I would hate it. As I read our history in Britain, and as I read the history of Israel, everything depended on whether there was a good king or a bad king, and I can define them. A good king is someone who is first of all concerned about his subjects – their protection and wellbeing. A bad king is someone who is primarily concerned with his own status, power or wealth. You can find history is strewn with good kings and bad kings. A bad king will lay a heavy burden on his subjects because he has to pay for all his activities.

A good king will lay light burdens on his subjects. Hear the words of Jesus: "My burden is light...." He is telling us that he is a good king. In Jesus' kingdom there are more benefits than burdens, whereas in a bad king's kingdom there are more burdens than benefits. Would you really like to live in a country where one man made all the laws and there was no election, no votes and you had no choice? There is something to be said for benevolent dictatorship. We were not made for democracy. I read a lovely comment that during World War 2 we fought to make the world safe for democracy and then discovered democracy was not safe for the world. That is a cynical remark, but the fact is that you and I were not made to run our own lives – we crave leadership.

One of the things I have noticed in modern politics is that invariably it is a contest about the leadership. We pin messianic hopes on the leader of a party. It is an impossible task to expect anyone to get us out of the mess we are in. It is asking too much and so we elect them and not long afterwards we are disillusioned and looking for another leader. Could you name six Government ministers? In Israel, which reflects the world situation so frequently, there was a swing from democratic government to kingdom government. The reason is that the early years of the State of Israel were dominated by Ashkenazi Jews from northern Europe and Western civilization – people like David Ben Gurion and Golda Meir. Their dream was of a social democracy. That changed. It became a dream of a strong king. The Sephardic Jews from the Orient came to have the major vote in Israel.

The Sephardic Jews had never lived in democracy– most of them lived in kingdoms.

I see God preparing the world for kingship again. Since 1914, twenty-four crowned heads of Europe have fallen. Kings have been disappearing like ninepins. Britain is one of the very few countries left that still has a notional royal family around. The world swung away from royalty to republicanism, and then I detected a swing back. People were looking again for authority, leadership. People are looking again for a king. They may not use that word but it is what deep in their hearts they want – and the reason is they were made for it.

So let me come right down to brass tacks. *We have been so accustomed to regarding God as Father that we have overlooked the fact that he is King.* Traditionally, when a Jew begins his meal, he calls God "King of the universe" and then thanks him.

The word "God" means someone who was always there and someone who is in total charge. In many languages of the world, the word "God" and the word "King" are the same word. In the ancient world there was no question about it: to say "God" was to say "King". The idea of a God who did not rule as well as reign would have been anathema.

Yet I believe that one of our biggest problems in Britain today is a view of God that has turned him into a constitutional monarch. What I mean by that is God is treated as the Queen is treated – not taken into account in daily life; not considered as actually in charge; not in control. The Bible opens with God as King. You have to read a long way through the Bible before you find God as Father. You have to read even further before you read that he is love. But the Bible begins with a picture of God as King sitting on a throne issuing commands, which are instantaneously and universally obeyed.

I made videotapes on the first three chapters of Genesis, just ten tapes that were a series of talks for Christians and their non-Christian neighbours to come in and watch. But the more I looked into the first three chapters, the more I realised that is where the battle still is. Genesis 1 has ten commandments in it – and they were obeyed, every one. God simply had to say it and it was done.

You have a picture in Genesis 1 and 2 of an entire universe subject to the sovereignty of God. Don't you get a feeling it must have been a beautiful world? What a place to live in – everything so good, so beautiful, with no disease, no death, no war, no famine; enough for every animal and every person to eat – a place that was not only useful but beautiful. I love the way that God realised that human beings didn't just need cabbages they needed flowers too – that we need beauty as well as usefulness. So he did not put us in an allotment but in a garden. He put the wild animals out in the field, but for man he planted a garden because we would appreciate beauty. Everything was beautiful – paradise. If only the world had stayed that way! The reason it was that way was that God was King. When he said, "Let there be light," there it was. He is sovereign, and everything was subject to his sovereignty and that was sheer heaven on earth. When we read the story of creation to our little daughter once, she sat back at the end and she said, "No sooner said than done, wasn't it?" What a beautiful response, a perfect analysis. God said, "Let the dry land appear," and there it was. He just had to issue a command and it was obeyed.

My wife and I, for the first time in our married life, acquired a home of our own. It was a lovely place with the most beautiful garden. We asked the Lord for a garden that would not require any looking after because we travel such a lot. He gave us the most beautiful garden that requires no digging, no weeding. It was all water! It had a large pond surrounded by trees, and our little house was on the edge of it. We had a number of ducks and moorhens, a couple of kingfishers and a few white doves. The whole pond was a spring of living water. So it did not become stagnant. We called the house "Still Waters" for obvious reasons.

As I sat in my study, looking out on this beautiful scene, I thought: why is it beautiful? The answer is: because everything I can see is subject to God. Then I turn on the television and listen to the news, or I read the newspaper, and it seems as if nothing is subject to God and it is ugly, horrible. Those clouds in the sky, and the hills, have to obey God, they have no choice. One of the reasons the surroundings we have are good for our souls is that you are looking at things that are subject to God. Evidence of his sovereignty is all around you. Now there are many people who believe that God may have created all this but that he no longer controls it.

I want to give you two philosophical terms now: deism and theism. The greatest enemy of God in this land is not atheism, it is deism, so I had better explain what I mean. Deism is the belief that God created all things but no longer controls them. A deist believes God made this universe like a watch, wound it up, and now it operates according to its own laws.

A Methodist lay preacher who was a meteorologist got the figures for me about the rain that fell on Israel for the last 150 years, and you can actually plot the political history of Israel from the rainfall chart. It is extraordinary. Every time there was an *aliyah*, a new wave of immigration of Jews to Israel, the rainfall went up. But the meteorologist could not see that God is in control. Israel's rainfall reached the all-time record for a century in the spring of 1948. To a Jew that is no problem at all. In fact, when the first *aliyah* took place, between 1872 and 1875, the rain fell as it had not fallen for centuries, and the rabbis fell on the ground and praised the King of the universe because he had restored the rain. But how many people – today, in this country – really believe that God is in total control of the weather? I am almost bold enough to say that every time you complain about the weather you become a deist! You are saying God is not in control, or if you think he is in control you are saying you do not like the way he is running things.

The big question is whether we are deists or theists. Many people in Britain believe in God but most are deists, not theists. The important question is not whether you believe in God but what kind of a God you believe in. Do you believe in the living God or not?

Some years ago I took part in a televised discussion on the question: does God answer prayer by performing miracles today? When my wife and I arrived at the studio and we went into the reception room for the guests who would be appearing on the show, we were introduced – horror of horrors – to about twenty people, all of whom were going to take part in the twenty-five minute discussion. I had thought there were going to be three or four speakers. Some quick mental arithmetic suggested I would have three-quarters of a minute to speak! What could I say in forty-five seconds? We were introduced to the rest of the guests. There was a punk rocker who, as far as we could see, was held together with safety pins. There was a housewife, a teacher, a real live bishop (I speak physically) and an ex-Moderator of the Church of Scotland. There was a well-known evangelical professor who had published many books. I was relieved when the door opened and Colin Urquhart walked in, and felt there was someone there with a fellow opinion. But they introduced me to a man of about fifty in a bright red shirt who was said to be the President of the British Humanist Association.

We went into the studio and sat down in the second row of a tiered platform. Immediately in front of me was the humanist (the evangelical professor on one side of him and the bishop on the other). Colin and I looked down and noticed that the humanist had by his side a pile of newspaper cuttings from the Sunday gutter press. Horrible stuff – the top one was about a poor girl pummelled to death by two misguided young men trying to get a demon out of her. Clearly, the chairman had all these dreadful, scandalous stories to attack Christianity. They were not on the subject but he had come well-armed and well-prepared. So I nudged Colin and said, "We've just time to pray," and before the programme began we prayed, "In the name of the Lord Jesus, we bind those newspaper articles so that he can't even use them." Then the red light lit up on the camera and we were on air.

The chairman turned to the evangelical professor and said, "Now what do you think about this, professor?" The professor was very nervous and he jumped. He knocked over a glass of water, which fell on the newspaper articles and stuck them to the floor. When the humanist tried to get those newspaper articles they came away in shreds and he was picking at them with his little fingernail. I can see him now! He couldn't get them up and they were just ripped to pieces. While this was happening the chairman turned to me and said, "Now we've got David Pawson with us. What do you think? Do you think that God answers prayer today?" The frustration was that I couldn't point to the articles because I didn't want to draw attention to them. So I told the story of a friend of mine, a building contractor who was as tough as they come – it was said of him that the softest part of him was his teeth. But then he was converted and became like a little child. Late one night he had a telephone call from a friend of his who lived three hundred miles away. The friend just said, "Bill, I want to say goodbye and thank you."

He said, "What do you mean? Where are you going?"

"Well," he said, "I'm going to end it all. You're the only man who has ever helped me so I want to say thank you, but the business has collapsed, my marriage has collapsed and I have nothing to live for – so goodbye."

My friend Bill replied, "Stay there, don't do a thing. I'm coming straight to you." He dashed out to get his car, and he set off to drive to save this man's life. He got seventy-five miles into the country and the car stopped. He looked at the petrol gauge and it was against empty, and he kicked himself. Why did he set out without looking? He waited for cars to come along the road, but none came. He looked around but there was not a light in sight, it was such a remote spot. So, being a very new Christian, he prayed. Then he shook the car to try to get some petrol to the engine. He managed to get it going again. He set off once more and a few hours later he drove into the drive of the man who had phoned him, having not stopped in 275 miles on an empty tank. He saved the man's life and he saved his soul.

As soon as I had finished saying that (in three-quarters of a minute), the humanist turned to the bishop and said, "Do you believe that bishop?"

The bishop said, "Well, I have a different view of prayer to David Pawson. For me, prayer is not asking for things, it's communing with the Almighty." The humanist sneered, the corner of his lip turned up. At the end of the programme the humanist turned around and he said to Colin and myself, "You two are genuine. I don't believe a word you've said but you obviously believe that God still answers prayer." Then he pointed at the bishop and at the evangelical professor and at the ex-Moderator of the Church of Scotland and said, "They don't believe, do they?" What do you say then? I think you have got to be honest with the world and I said, "No they don't, but some of us still do."

Now what had he spotted? He spotted that there is a division line right through the church, right through the clergy, between those who believe in God and those who believe in the *living* God; those who view him as Father but who have not understood him as King, and those who believe he is the Father in heaven *and* the King over the universe, and still in charge. That is the difference between deism and theism. If there is one thing that the Renewal has done, it has turned thousands of deists into theists. An atheist is not an a-deist. An atheist may not be someone who doesn't believe in God but someone who does not believe he is in charge. It is that kind of atheism that is our problem.

Let us go a little further. I know I am being critical of the church. It is as one who identifies with the church and who wants to wake up the church. Many years ago, a Doctrine Commission of the Church of England was the subject of media attention. A bishop appeared on television and said, "We must see that God needs our help, that he is as weak as water," and he used that phrase deliberately – twice. The bishop's line was that the world is a mess because God needs us to help him out. He portrayed a God to be pitied rather than worshipped; not a God who was in charge, not the King of the universe. So the interviewer, who was not a Christian, said, "But aren't we to think of God as Father?" and the bishop replied, "Well, you see, I like to think of a large family held together by a grandmother in the family whose affection for everybody holds the thing together." Is God a grandmother? That is near blasphemy.

When I read the Bible I do not find a God who, having created all this, left it to run itself. The Bible is theistic from cover to cover. It talks of a God who is King and who still reigns, and I want to start there because we need to get the clear faith in our hearts that God is in total control of the situation – that whatever we do we cannot stop God's kingdom coming; that this world has not got out of hand; that he still reigns.

A little girl went home from Sunday school singing a chorus she had learned, "God is still on the phone; God is still on the phone." That is about where many people's faith is – thinking he is just someone to talk to when you are in trouble. But God is still on the *throne*.

Have you ever realised that through the Bible God is presented as in control of every level of creation? He is in control of the wind, the snow, the waves of the sea, the frost and the rain. During one dreadful winter of snow and ice, this was a word that I was reading and preaching from at the time: "God's voice thunders in marvellous ways. He does great things beyond our understanding. He says to the snow, 'fall on the earth,' and to the rain shower, 'be a mighty downpour' so that all men he has made may know his work. He stops every man from his labour." What a passage! I found it a great joy to preach it during that winter when England was paralysed and nobody could go to work for days. Industries seemed to come to a halt because of snow.

The Bible says: so that you can remember my work, I'll stop yours with snow. That is a vivid concept of God as King – God in total charge. Which is the biggest miracle in the book of Jonah, the whale or the worm? Have you ever asked yourself that? In the early chapters of Jonah, God sends a whale. In the last chapter he sends a worm. Which is the bigger miracle? Well you try training a whale and you try training a worm. According to the Bible, God is in total control of frogs, flies, whales and worms.

Forgive me if this sounds like Sunday school teaching, but every part of creation is under his total control, whether it is the weather or any creature he has made. When they brought the ark back to Jerusalem they hitched it to some oxen that had never had a yoke on them but they went the right way by themselves. I think of Jesus riding on an ass that no man had ever sat on. Have you ever tried doing that? I used to break in horses on the farm, and you try sitting on something that no man has sat on, everything under perfect control! You find that God is in complete control of history as well as nature in the Bible. No matter how pagan or how evil a man may be, God is in total control. That is why I like the biblical account of Nebuchadnezzar, the man who thought he was "it". "Is not this great Babylon, which I have built as my kingdom for my power and my glory?" Nebuchadnezzar then became like an animal,with great fingernails and unkempt hair, eating grass like an ox. Later, his sanity returned and he acknowledged that God is in charge.

I want you to get a sense that God is in complete control. He is King of the universe no matter what he has made. He never left it to run on its own, he is still in charge. Therefore the God of the Bible is still the God who is, and he is the God known to believers (Christian theism – not deism). Any miracle you read in the Bible he could do today – or he would not be God.

People say, "But what about the laws of nature?" I will tell you what I think of the laws of nature. I think they are like the headmaster's timetable, which he can alter any time he likes. What we call the laws of nature are God's habits and God can change them at his pleasure.

In Australia I worked with a Nigerian man whose faith I envied. It was so naïve. Do you know what I mean by that? In Western civilization, many are so sophisticated that they can't cope with miracles. But this Nigerian arrived in Australia with archbishop's flowing robes and a mighty cross around his neck. When he got to the immigration authorities in Sydney they said, "Where's your visa? You've got to have a visa now to get into Australia."

He said, "I haven't time to bother with visas."

They said, "Well you can't come in here then."

He said, "I have as much right to be here as you have."

They said, "What right have you to be here?"

He replied, "This is my father's country."

"Let him in," they said, and he came in. He had been led to the Lord by an elderly missionary when he was twenty-three when he did not even have a pair of shoes. He had no worldly possessions but a pair of shorts. Soon after he became a Christian and had read his New Testament, he said to the old missionary, "It says here that Jesus raised the dead."

The missionary said, "That's right."

So he asked, "How many dead have you raised?"

The missionary said, "Well, not many lately," or words to that effect.

"But you said that Jesus was the same today?"

"Yes." So he got on his bicycle on that Sunday morning and went around the city, knocking at doors, asking, "Is there anybody dead in here?" He couldn't find anybody till half past four that afternoon. Hearing weeping and wailing coming from a house, he knocked at the door and said, "Somebody died here?"

"Yes we're just about to have the funeral," came the reply.

He said, "No need it's alright," and he went in. There was a little girl in her coffin. He asked, "How long has she been dead?"

"Since nine o'clock this morning, so we've got to get the funeral over soon. We're just about to screw the lid on." But he lifted that little body out of the coffin, cuddled her, and he prayed for her. She sneezed. He gave her back to her parents. He went on like that until he had raised six people, then reported back to the missionary. I envy someone with naïve faith. Everything about our environment here teaches us to regard God as a constitutional monarch who isn't really in charge.

Get it firmly in your mind: God is not as weak as water. He is not a helpless, disappointed person in heaven who says, "I wanted to do them good but I couldn't." God is not dependent on us, we are dependent on him. His sovereignty! He could blot this whole world out tomorrow, and as Martin Luther said, "If I had been God I would have kicked the world to pieces long ago." We must never think that the patience of God is his weakness, nor should we allow the fact that he allows us astonishing freedom to obscure from us the fact that he has set limits.

Those who believe that God is King – that his dominion is an everlasting dominion, and that his kingdom is an everlasting kingdom; that he is on the throne – are those who believe in miracles. They are those who believe in the *living* God. They are those who believe that he is talking and acting today. I finish this chapter where I began: *God is looking for subjects*. There is nothing wrong with his sovereignty; his arm is not shortened. He is looking for subjects who will be his kingdom on earth. He has chosen a different way from the one we would have chosen to re-establish paradise.

2

THE KINGDOM OF SATAN

For six days in 1967 I watched television non-stop and came to realise that God is the Lord of history and the King of the nations, and that history is "his story". It was the Six-Day War in which Israel had that amazing victory. I knew as I watched the screen that you could not explain that victory in human terms alone. I went out to Israel immediately after the war and was up on the Golan Heights with an Israeli army Major. I saw the rows of Russian guns and the wrecked Russian tanks. Looking down on the valley, I said to the Major, "How on earth could you possibly take this hill? How could you get up here in the face of all that?" He answered simply by pointing his finger to the sky and I knew what (or who) he meant.

By 1973, Israel had become proud. They thought they had done it themselves. I remember watching the victory parade on "May Day" or the day of independence of the State of Israel. As I watched the proud parade of the Israeli troops, I remember turning to someone and saying, "God will have to do something to humble this people." A few months later (Yom Kippur, October 1973) the Arabs marched and Israel's pride was smashed. You see God's hand in history – both in victory and in defeat. So it was from 1967 that I began to think of God as the King of the nations.

George Thomas, former Speaker of the House of Commons and a very God-fearing man, said on his retirement that when he mentioned God in the Commons he felt old-fashioned. That was quite a comment on our Parliament.

George Thomas invited me to address members of both Houses of Parliament, and I spoke to them about God's ancient people Israel. I showed them how six British prime ministers in my lifetime had gone into the political wilderness within days or weeks of breaking faith with the people of God called "Israel". From Neville Chamberlain to Winston Churchill in 1945; Anthony Eden, right through to James Callaghan. One prime minister, who not only kept every promise but stayed faithful to that people, at risk to his own life and contrary to the advice of those around him, had the longest term in office of any prime minister in the twentieth century and was not voted out when he decided to retire, and that was Harold Wilson. I am not now taking political sides but I am pointing out a very real factor.

After I had said these things to members of both Houses of Parliament I remember a prominent Member of Parliament getting up, his face red with anger. He said, "What about freewill? I am here because I chose to be an MP. I am here because my constituents chose me as their member." I said, "You have free will, so have your constituents. But God has more freewill than you have, and God has the casting vote in any election." The thought that God was in charge of the British government was anathema to that man. He resented the idea that God decides the result of elections. He resented the idea that God chose and "un-chose" prime ministers of Britain. In fact, the human heart rebels against any idea that God is in charge. When you uncover the hearts of many MPs there is a sheer resentment against the belief in the kingdom of God.

Now we must explore the strange contradictions between faith and facts, or rather between what we believe and what we see. This world does not look as if it is under the complete control of God, does it? There are many things happening in our world that are very difficult to explain if you believe that God is in control. I start with one of the most difficult, and that is the subtle shift in world climate in 1971, which has narrowed all the rain belts of our globe and led to the situation where many countries suffer appalling drought and others suffer floods. There has been a redistribution of rainfall since 1971. The meteorologists cannot explain it, but it has caused widespread suffering. So it is not just in political affairs but in natural affairs that it may not look as if God is in charge. When I say that God is on the throne and in total control of the situation I am speaking by faith, but I did not read it in this morning's newspaper. I believe it but I do not see it. When I look at the violence, when I hear of wars, rumours of wars, famines and earthquakes, what I see tells me that the thing is out of control. This contradiction between what we believe and what we see has to be faced very honestly and explained.

There are two explanations that I want to reject. One is that God is a bad king and is mismanaging the universe. The other is that he is a weak king and cannot do any more about it than we can. Those two explanations are quite widely held. Every time somebody says, "Why does God allow that?" they are implying that he is a bad king, or a weak king. Every time people complain that God should have stopped this, started that or done the other, they are implying he is not a good king.

Now when you believe in the God of the Bible you cannot possibly explain this apparent contradiction in terms of God being a bad king. Every page, from the very first, tells us that "good God" is the essence of our theology. When people ask me to speak and they want a title months before I arrive, I never know what to say, so I usually reply, "Well, tell them I'll speak on 'Good God'." That covers all my theology and everything I want to say. It is fundamental to the Bible that God is good and that therefore everything he does is good.

It has got to be. Of everything he made with his hands, he said, "That's good; that's a good job." When he made you and me he said, "That's very good." The thought that the world is in a mess because God is bad is unthinkable to the Christian. Many years ago a man said to me, "The world is in a hell of a mess, isn't it?" I said, "If you're using that word as I would use it, you are not far off the truth."

What about the explanation that God is a *weak* king, which is now being touted by bishops: that poor old God needs our help because he is looking at the world and wringing his hands – that he doesn't know what to do with it? That is not the concept of God as a good king, but many people have come to believe that God is weak, that he is helpless in the face of the many things that are happening in our world and cannot stop them, and really is a very disappointed, frustrated God. That is not the answer.

What then is the answer to this mess which the world is in? For the last four thousand years of history there have only been three hundred years of peace with no major war taking place. Let that sink in. In my lifetime, millions have been slaughtered. More people died violently in Russia than in the whole of World War II. We live in a dreadful world and here we are, we go out to that world and we say, "God is on the throne; God is in control; God has the last word." People say, "It doesn't measure up. I can't figure it out. He's a funny sort of God to let all this happen."

The third explanation is the one the Bible gives, namely that part of God's creation was given the vote. Not the vote to vote him in or out, but the vote to vote themselves in or out. To two parts of God's creation God gave the power of the vote: to the human race and to the angelic host. The Bible is absolutely clear that the whole of the human race, and a third of the angelic host, exercised their vote to opt out of being subject to the King. The explanation of the mess we are in lies in the remarkable tolerance of God in allowing that to take place. He must have known it would happen.

If you don't understand that God is a prodigal Father you had better read the Bible again. I call the story in Luke 15 "the parable of the prodigal father". Why? Because he gave his sons the money—astonishing. He must have known what the younger son would do with it but he gave him the money. What a prodigal father! I am amazed at what God has allowed me to do. He could have stopped me at any point, yet he let me do it. He is the prodigal Father, the King, who for reasons best known to himself has decided that part, at least, of his creation should have the vote to opt out of his kingdom. I believe the basic reason why he did that was that his heart was for voluntary subjects, for those who were not forced to do his will. He got pleasure out of the mountains, the winds, the hills, the waves, the animals, the birds, because they had to do his will. They gave him pleasure and he created all things for his pleasure. But he knew that he could never get the same pleasure from beings or creatures that were forced to be his subjects as he would have from those who voluntarily said, "We accept your sovereignty." That, I believe, lies at the heart of the mystery of the mess.

We find right at the beginning of the Bible that man was faced with a choice. He was offered the sovereignty of all that God had made. Consider this planet—the astronauts who went to the moon said that this planet was the most beautiful thing they saw. I remember one of the astronauts coming to our home for a meal, and just to talk with a man who has played golf on the moon is quite an experience! Incidentally, that man was the man who took sin to the moon. I don't know if you know the story, but he decided to smuggle aboard the lunar module hundreds of stamps, which he was going to frank or stamp on the moon and he knew he could sell them for a thousand dollars each when he got back home. They were not allowed on that trip, but he managed to smuggle hundreds of stamps which he was going to sell to philatelists when he returned. He discovered that philately will get you nowhere! In fact, on the moon while he cancelled those stamps, he was convicted of sin. He came back to earth and went straight and got baptized to get clean in God's sight. But I remember him telling us that the sight of planet earth as they came back was beautiful. Here is the only planet in the whole universe, as far as we know, that is two-thirds water, which is fundamental to our life. It is indeed a beautiful planet – it is green; packed with life. Just a handful of soil is packed with life. God was delegating sovereignty to man, as far as creation goes. Those animals, those birds, the whole lot was to be ours. He told man to rule over it, control it, fill it, inhabit it, garden it, look after it – but the thing was: it is yours provided you are my subjects, and provided you acknowledge my sovereignty; it will not be a heavy burden, it just means out of all the trees there is one you don't touch.

I remember a young man in the RAF coming to me when I was a chaplain and saying, "What about the story I've just read about the Garden of Eden – is that true?" I replied, "Listen, suppose I put you in a library where there were thousands of fascinating books, more than you could read in your lifetime, and then imagine I left you alone in that library and you noticed that on the top shelf there was a book which said, 'Not to be read by anyone under twenty-one.' I leave you alone in that library; there are all the books you could ever enjoy, what are you going to do?" He grinned and said, "I guess it must be true." He realised it was true of him – something in human nature says "I will not be told."

I am sure you have discovered with your children, as somebody wrote to me: "The trouble with having children is that you see your own faults developing in them." Did you notice that your child learned to say no before they learned to say yes? Did you notice that you never had to teach them to be dishonest, only to be honest? Did you notice that you never had to teach them to be cruel, only to be kind? Did you notice you never had to teach them how to hide things from you, but you had to wheedle things out of them to share with you? Why? We have to go back to the very beginning and realise the simple truth that there are in fact two kingdoms here on earth, and that we are involved in a mortal conflict between them. We do not start life innocent. However nice that little baby looks, the simple fact is it was born in the wrong kingdom, and you are a fool if you think otherwise.

There is a dreadful verse in the New Testament (which also says that we know we belong to God): that we know that the whole world lies in the control of the evil one. Do you know that? The previous verse, by the way, is equally challenging. It says, "Whoever is born of God does not go on sinning." So one of the marks of someone who has been born again, a subject of the kingdom of God, is that he or she does not go on sinning. In other words, the church is not a home for incurables, it is a hospital for sinners – but it turns out saints.

Let us now go right back to man saying, in effect: "God, I don't want to be a tenant on planet earth, I want to be landlord. I resent being a subject, I resent being told what to do." There are two ways to moral experience. One is to allow yourself to be a subject and to be told what is right and wrong without sampling them. The other is to say, "I won't have you telling me what to do, I will taste these things and I will decide for myself what is good for me and what is bad for me." The Bible teaches us that from the beginning that second choice was the one the human race made. You see every generation making it.

I can remember my first cigarette. I would have been about

ten and a half years old. I could take you to the bush where I hid and where we smoked a pack. I had been told not to; I had been told it would be bad for me, but I was jolly well going to find out. I found out and I was pretty sick. I had tasted it and found it was not good for me. From one point of view I am grateful I did because I have never wanted a cigarette since and it is not one of my temptations.

I have discovered this, and you will discover it too, that you can never know good and evil as God knows them. God knows good first hand and evil secondhand. When you have tried both you will know evil first hand and good secondhand. What do I mean by that? I mean that if you are not willing to be subject, and to be told by someone else what is good and evil, you lose your innocence and you can never regain it. Let us take sex outside marriage. Many young people may have heard that it was wrong but have tried it. Some have found that outside of a loving loyal relationship it can be pretty stale or sour. It can even put someone off you.

You can never go back to the innocence you had before you took of the fruit of knowledge of good and evil. Many of us would love to go back and get our innocence in certain areas back again, but you can't. Even divine grace and forgiveness can never change your past. It can change your future, it can restore broken relationships, but it can never restore innocence. When the young man I call "the prodigal's son" came home, he did not get his money back. That was spent; it was gone. In other words, there are consequences of rebellion that you never get over. There are penalties, which can be forgiven, and that is a very important distinction. If I steal apples, eat them and then get stomach ache, that is a consequence. If I am punished for the theft of those apples then that is the penalty. Forgiveness can remove the penalty but it can't remove the consequence.

God's message was: I am to be sovereign, you are to be

subject, and you can have control but I retain the right to decide what is good and evil. You don't decide from your own experience. I will tell you what is good and evil and you are my subject and you don't touch that experience for yourself. That is the meaning of the Garden of Eden. It was a beautiful place, but that one tree stood for one thing: that God was sovereign and man was to be subject. Had it stayed that way it would have been Paradise. But I find still that right through the human race there is an attitude, "I'm not going to have God telling me what's right and wrong for me. I'll decide for myself. I'll try it and I'll decide afterwards." But you are prejudiced afterwards; you are marked afterwards; you are marred.

So we have all lost innocence. In fact, that means there is not one of us who is the person you or I might have been by now had we been subject to the will of God. There has only been one life ever lived in whom God was well-pleased. God knows what I could have been by now had I let him be sovereign in my life. The result is that the human race has set about building its own kingdoms—some of them big, some of them small.

What is your kingdom? It could be just your house and your garden. That is my little kingdom in which I do what I want and what I decide is good. Others have had overweening ambition to have the biggest kingdom of all. I am old enough to remember Hitler's ravings about the thousand year Reich—the kingdom.

Idi Amin had an ambition of the same sort – to have a kingdom, to be boss, to be the big person. You may be someone who is doing that within your own home and family. We want our own kingdoms.

Secondly, the result is that we decide we will have our own kind of gods. We call that "idolatry". Whether you make a god of wood or stone, or whether you just construct a god of your own imagination and say, "Well this is what I think God is like," that is manipulating God because you manipulate what you make. You have got "God" nicely bottled up in your own ideas. I meet many people who have idols – because when I tell them what God is really like they often say, "But I don't think God is like that – no, I think God is like this." For example, you tell them about hell and they reply, "Oh, I don't think God would ever send anybody to hell, except someone like Hitler." No? That is their idea of God.

In fact, I would dare to say that many people's idea of God is of a grandfather rather than a father. That is their image of God: a nice old boy who wants us to be happy, pats us on the head and says, "We'll forgive and forget. Now what can I do for you next?" That is not the picture of God in the Bible, it is an idol. Once you make an image of God, once you make your own idea of God, once you fashion God according to what you think he should be like, the very next step is immorality, which always follows idolatry because you then bend the rules. You start saying, "Well, this is what I think is right and this is what I think is wrong."

My wife and I had an interesting experience at Lincoln showground many years ago. I was speaking to a large gathering of young people one August bank holiday. We had a staff room where we relaxed between sessions. I went through to this room and somebody said, "There's a couple here, and the man wants to talk to you." So I was introduced. A very godly woman had brought this man along, and I think they were neighbours. She said, "He wants to challenge you." He turned out to be a convinced left wing radical socialist. He really believed that was the answer and that he was devoting his life to a cause that would change the world. He said he wanted to help mankind and at last he said, "I feel I've found the real answer." He felt that what I had been saying was quite beside the point and irrelevant. The man was sincere and it is great to meet somebody who really wants to make this world a little better, rather than just look after himself and his family. But nevertheless the Lord led me to say something to him, which was this, "Stealing is stealing, and you either play by the rules or you don't." I had no idea that that was to be God's word that touched his inmost soul. He did not show anything at the time, but he went away from me. It was one of those encounters when you think, "Did I get through at all? Did I say anything to him?" He went and sat in the main hall. He later wrote to me: "It was as if I was a little sheep and a shepherd came and clipped me and I just was shorn of everything." He was blown apart, and the Lord met him because of that statement, "stealing is stealing" – it touched him with one of God's laws of his kingdom, because with all his humanitarianism, with all his socialism, with all his desire to better mankind, in God's sight he was a thief, and he had justified it to himself. He was saying, in effect, "It's all right. In the situation we are in today it's all right to take that from the firm," or whatever it was. But God touched him. He signed the letter, "Late of planet earth." I thought: as a man free from the kingdom of earth, he is in the kingdom of heaven.

We used to talk in the UK about "UDI" and that meant "Unilateral Declaration of Independence", which was what happened in the country then called Rhodesia. Declaring UDI against God, we say: "Right, God, from now on I decide for myself." Most people decide for themselves what is good and what is bad and what they will do. The next step is that they have to construct an idol; they have to fill the God-shaped blank with a "god" of their own idea. The next step is to bend the rules because if you can make a god whom you can manipulate, you can then manipulate the Ten Commandments any way you like, and you can make your own rules for yourself. The serious side of all this is that wherever there is an atmosphere of rebellion against authority, that actually allows room for a strong man to come in with a much more burdensome kingdom. Time and again you hear of countries where there has been a revolution in the name of freedom and they have finished up with a worse dictatorship than before the revolution. Why? Because where there is an atmosphere of rebelling against any authority, an authoritarian leader will get his chance to come in and offer to bring order out of the chaos that has resulted—that is the pattern of history.

We live in a world and I live in a nation where there is an atmosphere of rebellion against authority, starting with the home, which is where the first breakdown of authority occurs. But I tell you this: no government can keep its authority in a nation where parental authority has gone. Once parental authority goes, every other authority will collapse sooner or later. What does that leave? It leaves a vacuum and I tremble.

We are getting a polarised situation in which we could finish up with either a radical right or a radical left promising to bring us out of our troubles. In fact that will exactly be the strategy of Antichrist, who will promise to bring peace and security to a chaotic world. Where there is rebellion against authority some strong power will get in there. Human beings have said to God, "We will not have you reign over us. We will not obey your commandments. We will decide what is right and wrong. We will decide about marriage, we will decide about life, we will decide all these things."

What happened? Satan got his chance. It is not that we got our freedom, we just got ourselves into another kingdom where the burdens far outweighed the benefits. We accepted another sovereignty – other than that of God – but we did not guess the price of subjection to that other sovereign.

I regard Satan as the great "drug pusher". That is his

method. He offers in his sovereignty anything we want: any pleasure we want, any power we want, any fame we want. They are his to give, too. Since he controls this world he can offer you anything in this world you want. But the price you pay is an addiction which enslaves you to him. He even tried it on Jesus. He said, "I'll give you all the kingdoms of the world if...." Did you notice that Jesus didn't quarrel and say, "But they are not yours to give"? Jesus never took Satan lightly. He was not going to be Satan's subject. Jesus served only one King and he was not accepting the kingdoms of the world on Satan's terms. Most of us do, and Satan knows this inside out, and he can suggest to us: "If this is what you want I'll give it to you. Just bow down and serve me."

Let us backtrack a bit. Unless you realise that there is a higher order of intelligent life in the universe than man, you will not make sense of all this. Have you noticed that no evolutionist ever talks about angels? Because they just do not fit the scheme. Angels did not evolve from man so your evolutionist cannot cope with angels. So modern man, when rejecting God and rejecting angels, is left with an empty universe. We feel desperately lonely in an empty universe. The thought that we are the only beings in the entire universe who can talk to each other is horrifying. So what do we do? We think we are at the top of the ladder of life, and we then feel so lonely that we have to start populating outer space with creatures of our own imagination! Science fiction is very popular. When a Russian cosmonaut went into space and came back, he was asked if he had seen any angels. He said, "No I didn't see any," but they saw him. An American astronaut was nearer the truth when he was asked, "Did you meet God?" He replied, "No, but if I had stepped out of my spacesuit I would have done!" This universe is populated through and through. There is an intelligent life above us but below God. Not only was the human race given the vote to vote themselves out of the kingdom of God, but that higher order of beings we call "angels" was also given the vote. That higher order of beings took advantage of our rebellion to establish control on planet earth. That is the biblical explanation of the mess we are in. We have been invaded from outer space. There are thousands of people who are possessed by intelligent life that is not their own, and they need deliverance, they are in another kingdom.

I would tremble to talk about the kingdom of Satan if Christ were not present. Never laugh at the devil. If you make fun of him, you are in his group. Treat him very seriously indeed. Whenever I have spoken about Satan I get conscious of being involved in a battle. Some of the tape recordings I have made about him have been more interfered with electronically than any other recordings I have made. So I do not underestimate Satan, but he is not God. He is not omnipotent, not omniscient and not omnipresent. Omnipotent means all-powerful, able to do anything; omniscient means knowing everything; omnipresent means being everywhere at the same time. God has all those three attributes, but Satan does not. One of the biggest mistakes that Christians make is to think that Satan is everywhere at the same time. He is not – he is an angel. He can only be in one place at a time. Sometimes you might get a bit big-headed if you think Satan is giving you exclusive attention. I don't know where he is at this moment but I do know that, according to the Bible, Satan is the head of his kingdom and he has agents everywhere – and mostly what you experience is one of his agents. When God said once to Satan, "Where have you been?" the reply was, "Going to and fro in the earth." Satan can travel with the speed of light, but he can't be everywhere at once, so he uses agents. Many people think he is omnipresent, and therefore with them in the train, the office or wherever they are. Don't fool yourself, he is just an angel so he can only be in one place at once. But he can travel through the air quicker than a supersonic aeroplane – he is prince of the power of the air – but he runs a kingdom and here I want to concentrate on this.

There are two errors that Christians make in relation to Satan. One is to blame him for everything, as if all that goes wrong is personally to be attributed to him. That is to treat him far too lightly, not as a king. In fact, I remember somebody saying to me, "Satan has been getting at me all today."

"Tell me," I replied

"Well," he said, "I got up late, I rushed my breakfast and that gave me indigestion, then I missed the train at the station (I saw it pull out just as I got there). I arrived late at the office and I missed an important engagement."

I asked, "Why did you get up late?"

"I forgot to set the alarm last night."

I said, "None of what you have told me has anything to do with Satan."

Be careful about using him as a scapegoat for your own mistakes, folly or weakness. We really can't blame everything on Satan. That is to get it wrong. A lot of the trouble we get into is our own fault and we did it by our own foolishness, our own mistakes, our own sins.

The opposite error is to limit the work of Satan to too narrow a field. One of the dangers that Christians are in right now is that they think that Satan's work is almost exclusively occultism, spiritism, dabbling in black magic, and so on. Therefore many Christians make the mistake of thinking: I have never used a Ouija board and I have never gone to a medium, so I am all right. Don't you believe it. Satan is much more subtle than just to try and get people with Ouija boards—that is a more blatant and crude way. Certainly among unbelievers it is an increasingly common way for him to get hold of people. They do it first for a bit of fun, and then they find they are hooked. They read their horoscope for fun until it says something that fits, and then they wonder. They are playing with fire. But if you think that Satan only deals with black magic and occultism you are making a big mistake also. You have made his influence too narrow, as those who blame everything on him are making his influence too wide. So let me explain a few more things about this creature. He is an angel who decided that instead of being a subject like the other angels he would be a king. He chose, as the place to be king, this world. He persuaded a third of his fellow angels to join him in the conspiracy. Therefore he controls this world through those agents. He operates far more commonly in both the world and in the church than we realise. One of the urgent needs of today is not only that people come to faith in the kingdom of God, but that they also come to faith in the kingdom of Satan. Not faith in terms of trusting, but faith in terms of believing there is such a kingdom, and learning to recognise it.

I believe Satan has done more damage in the church than in the world. His deception has done more to hold this world in his chains. His deception among clergy has done terrible damage to the world because I believe the church is responsible for the state of the world. Do you believe that? I don't have sympathy with Christians who point at the world and say, "What a wicked world you are." What else could they be since they don't know God? We know God and we could have done something about that and prevented it. I believe God holds his people responsible for the state of the nation in which he has placed them. Therefore, it is we who need to repent for the nation, the nation can't repent for itself.

So let us look further into the kingdom of Satan. He is a king. Jesus called him the prince of this world, the ruler of this world. Paul calls him the god of this world. Those are very big titles to give. Don't have anything to do with the idea of Satan as a little imp with a fork in his hand and a forked tail, running around in a red jump suit. If the devil appeared like that to me I would have no problems. If someone looking like that knocked at my front door I would slam it in his face. Incidentally, Satanists have turned up in Christian meetings, usually all in black, giving the show away straightaway. Satan is more subtle than that. He is a master of disguise. He can dress up as an angel of light, or come to you even through your own nearest relative or friend, and you may not know it. So he runs a kingdom and he is a liar, a murderer, a killer; he is the father of lies – he hates.

Until you came to believe in God you probably did not believe in the devil either. But if you really met the Lord, you met the devil too. Do you know why? Because the devil is not in hell, he is in heaven. As soon as you get through to heavenly places in Christ, you will meet the spiritual hosts of wickedness in heavenly places—that is serious. It means the holier you get, the better your prayer life, the more likely you are to wrestle with principalities and powers. So far from thinking that it is those dreadful people who play with Ouija boards who have most problems with Satan, it is the saints who have most problems and I think we need to realise this. At every point at which you are likely to become a better subject of the kingdom you will have problems from the kingdom of Satan. It will probably be through one of his agents called demons, evil spirits.

Why is it such a battle for some people to get converted? When they are getting near the kingdom, when they are getting near to Christ, it seems somebody the other side of them is pulling hard. Have you had that experience? It becomes a tug-of-war. I remember a couple coming to lunch with us. I am afraid I was rather showing off by telling a story of going up a river in Kenya where the crocodiles were all around. We were sitting on a little hollowed out tree trunk, and I felt those crocodiles were too near. The wife of the couple who were having lunch with us just capped the story beautifully. (The penalty for telling a story is that somebody else caps it with a better one!) She said, "Look at that scar," and between her thumb and forefinger was a scar running back in that web of skin. She continued, "You know how I got that? I was having a picnic by a river in Africa with my boyfriend, and I was washing up the dishes in the river afterwards. I had this big dinner plate in my hand and suddenly out of the water came a big crocodile jaw and went right on my hand." The boyfriend, with great presence of mind, grabbed her ankles and it was a tug-of-war between the boy and the crocodile for that girl. Because she had a dinner plate in her hand, the bottom teeth, the bottom jaw, could not grip. The top tooth had gripped in the skin, and eventually the boyfriend's pulling ripped the skin and she was free. Have you ever felt like that when you are trying to win someone for Christ – as if all hell is let loose on the other side of them, and everything conspires against? I tell you, Satan hates people getting converted. You are spoiling the strong man's goods. It is warfare. You are not trying to persuade someone that life would be a bit nicer with Jesus. You are rescuing them from hell. You see much evangelism is just, "Like to come along to our church? You'll have nice times there. Do nice things, meet nice people." That is not what it is about. It is about releasing victims from their chains. Unless we take the kingdom of Satan seriously, evangelism loses its cutting edge. It is just making nice people nicer.

Someone said something to me that sent a sword through my heart: "We were having lots of trouble over baptism, but we have agreed that it is not important so we are over that problem now." I felt hurt and wanted to say: baptism not important? Was it not important to Jesus? He made it so fundamental that he said, 'Go and make disciples of all nations, baptising them....' and then teaching them. Baptism was the one thing he singled out, the one thing they all did. I wrote an article in a well-known Christian magazine on baptism. I just tried to point out what the biblical meaning of it is. They received more correspondence about that article than on any other topic. There was letter after letter shooting me down in flames until, after seven months, the editor called a halt to the debate. Talking about baptism provoked argument, and behind the furore there is something demonic – there is the kingdom of Satan, who hates people to be baptised as voluntary subjects of the king. That is because it is a weapon to be used against him. It is not a matter of churchmanship, it is a matter of the kingdom. It is the very first thing you do when you become a subject: you submit to the Lord's will. Whether you like it or not, whether you get a blessing out of it or not is beside the point. He said, "Do it," and you do it. Forever afterwards you can say to Satan, "You have no dominion over me because I was buried with Christ in baptism."

Many people are robbed of any meaningful relationship with their baptism. I believe that one of the ideas that has been most damaging is that if you have Christian parents you are born into the kingdom. But the New Testament knows no way of being born into the kingdom. You can be *born-again* into the kingdom when you repent and believe. But this is an issue that Satan hates to be brought up. He can't bear it to be mentioned that baptism is a burial and a bath. It is a burial for those who have died and a bath for those who are dirty.

Satan cannot bear that to be done because it is so decisive for a subject of the kingdom that he will cause any argument, any controversy, any threat, to turn a person away from becoming a subject of the kingdom in that way. Now I am declaring this strongly, but I believe I am touching something that Satan hates me to mention. He wants us to say, "It's not important, let's just agree to differ, let's get on with the important things." Well, to Jesus it was so important that even though he was the only person who did not need to be baptised, at the age of thirty he said it is right to do what is right.

The next stage that Satan cannot bear in your life is when you are baptised with the Holy Spirit—when you are plunged or drenched in him. I don't care what terminology you use. When I went to New Zealand I was met by a group of ministers at the airport. I said, "Now are there any things I shouldn't say? Because I don't know New Zealand, and I've got a wonderful gift for putting my foot in my mouth!" They said, "Well, don't use the term, 'Baptised in the Holy Spirit'. It's a hot potato here. It causes much division."

So I asked the Holy Spirit what I should say instead, and he said, "Say 'drenched'." So I just said "Drenched in the Holy Spirit" and everybody smiled; nobody got upset. Actually it is a marvellous translation of the Greek word *baptizein*.

I learned later that there were some ten times as many sheep as people in New Zealand and the word "drench" is used in ordinary speech by the sheep farmers. So it was the right word. So if you object to being "baptised" in the Spirit, how about being drenched? Soaked? Plunged? Dipped? I don't care what term you use, but Satan hates that – and look what he has tried to do with the gift of tongues.

Every gift that comes down from above is good and perfect. Satan has managed to make that gift one of the things that people argue about, fear and muddle about. As if God really made a big mistake to pour out that gift on the Day of Pentecost. "What a blunder! God, you might have chosen love or something nice. Why choose that?" Have you noticed that in fact Satan doesn't trouble you all the time, but when you are on the verge of becoming a better subject of the King and submitting to something because you know God has told you – that is when he troubles you or sends along one of his agents.

The evidence of Satan in the world is not just in the growth of substance abuse. I see that science, education, the arts, entertainment, industry and politics all reflect his power in this world. It is not just in the perverted vices that you see Satan's authority. You can see his authority in every department of life. The New Testament is not playing with words when it says that the whole world lies in his control, so take it seriously. Learn to recognise the kingdom of Satan wherever he is exercising his authority. There is indication in the Bible that he does have agents specifically detailed to exercise his authority over nations – "princes" they are called, who rule over particular nations and control them. The book of Daniel makes that quite clear. We are up against a highly organised kingdom.

Here are some of the characteristics of his kingdom and they all seem to begin with the letter "d". I am not sure what the significance of that is – it may just be that I have a tendency to alliteration, which it has been said is the province of fools, poets and Plymouth brethren! I have found that the devil has a kingdom of darkness, disease, deception, division and death. Such dreadful things are his price.

Take that world of *darkness*. What does it mean to call Satan's kingdom the kingdom of darkness? It means that his kingdom always has things to hide. If there are things in your life that you have got to hide, then there is ground for Satan to get hold. I am bold now to say that one of his curses – inside the church as well as outside – is freemasonry, which is a work of darkness. If you have been involved in freemasonry I beg you to renounce it and to get all its influence out of your life. I said that in a mining town in Australia, and I did not know that the masons so controlled it that if you spoke against them you could not buy groceries at the supermarket. When I mentioned freemasonry there, I found out the churches were riddled with it. It is a work of darkness; it has got things to hide. If you speak out boldly, you will soon find that you are up against a kingdom of darkness and against things that do not want to be brought to the light, things that do not want to be publicly known. You can always tell what Satan has got hold of because you want to hide it. You don't want it exposed to the light.

It is a kingdom of *disease*. God never intended doctors and nurses. I don't know why we place that vocation so high. Have you noticed that we have a list of Christian careers, which are "right"? Missionaries are at the top, ministers come second, doctors and nurses third, teachers fourth – with trades union workers right at the bottom. Have you noticed how we grade what Christians could and should do? But God never intended doctors and nurses – it is a kind of standby; he had to sort of arrange it later. Then I suppose he never intended missionaries or ministers either! In heaven I will be out of a job because there won't be any need to teach people about God – you will see him face to face. But we have these grades. The kingdom of Satan is a kingdom of disease, and Jesus tackled disease from that point of view: "This woman whom Satan has had bound for eighteen years...."

It is a kingdom of *deception*, and I think that Satan does more damage in the church through deception than perhaps any other cause. It is a sobering thought that Evan Roberts said the Welsh Revival came to nothing because the saints were deceived very soon afterwards. I ask why many other revivals have frittered out so quickly. The answer is invariably that those who were caught up in the revival were deceived.

I want you to know that somebody who is baptised in the Holy Spirit is far more open to deception by the kingdom of

Satan than someone who has not been baptised in the Holy Spirit. Because you are now open to the supernatural; you are now open to words from beyond; you are now open to prophecy. Satan is a master at counterfeit. Wherever there is true prophecy he will hand in false prophecy. Wherever there is true healing he will put in false healing. Wherever there is anything real he will put in the counterfeit. But he never bothers to put the counterfeit where there is nothing real. What would be the point? I don't counterfeit half crown coins and there would be no point because the real ones have gone out of use. Therefore you find that wherever there is a true prophet like Jeremiah there may be dozens of false prophets all around him saying other things. Once you are open to prophecy you are open to false prophecy.

Now I say this not to put you off being baptised in the Spirit, but many people just get baptised in the Spirit because they want a bit more joy, they want healing or they want to be guided better. They don't realise that they are heading for the front line of warfare, and are often quite unready to deal with it. If you are going to be ready to deal with that spiritual warfare you have got to stay very close to the Bible and you must beware of texts quoted out of context. Satan can quote the Bible better than most of us, but he always quotes the text out of context, and therefore it becomes a pretext for his own ideas.

Another safeguard in this warfare against the kingdom of Satan, which as soon as you are baptised in the Spirit you are right into, is this: there is safety in numbers. Check out all your guidance, your visions and your prophecies. Let others decide, let others weigh and judge. A man came to me after being filled with the Spirit and actually tried to tell me that he had a word direct from the Lord that he must leave his wife and go with another woman. Now I didn't know whether to say "Rubbish" or "Blasphemy". It was a bit of both, but he was deceived.

We can all be deceived. One day I made a list of the warnings in the New Testament of how you can be deceived. Jesus was concerned that his disciples should not be deceived. Satan plays around with your mind and he will do it even by quoting texts, and here are some of them. First, "If you are a hearer of the Word but not a doer of it you're deceived." James tells you that. So if you listen to good Christian teaching and say, "Oh, wasn't it nice," and, "Thank you for the nice talk," and, "Very interesting," and you do nothing about it, you are deceived. You have got ground for Satan in your life.

"You're deceived," says the New Testament if you say, "I've got no sin. I don't need to go forward and ask for forgiveness. I've got nothing to put right." You are also deceived if you say you are entirely sanctified; if you say, "I can't sin in that, that's finished with." The battle will be on until your dying moments. If you think you are something when you are nothing, you are deceived. If you think you are wise when you are foolish, you are deceived. If you say or think you are religious when your tongue is unbridled, you are deceived. I am just quoting from the New Testament here. If you think you won't reap what you have sown, you are deceived. If you think that you can go on in sin and inherit the kingdom, you are deceived. If you think that contact with bad company won't affect you, you are deceived. I have noticed that again and again the scripture addresses saintly Christians: "Don't be deceived."

Satan seems to be able to twist doctrine, to unbalance it, to over-emphasise one thing at one extreme to the exclusion of the balancing truth in scripture. Here is an example: the idea that Christians won't ever see the big trouble, that somehow they will just be caught out of it all and be wafted on the first bus to heaven before any trouble hits them. I believe that is a deception. It started in a prophesying meeting in Port Glasgow, Scotland and it has now gone around the world. It seems to have bemused Americans particularly. I have searched my Bible and I cannot find it there. No Christian ever found it in the Bible for eighteen centuries. If it was there they would surely have found it as Christians have searched for it, but it came out of prophesying. From Port Glasgow it went down to Albury House near Guildford, Surrey, and from there it went around the world. If I am wrong I would rather be wrong my way and tell you to get ready for trouble than in the other way.

I believe we have got to test and test and test these things lest the children of God be deceived. Jesus said in the last days there will be false prophets. There will be counterfeit miracles because the devil can counterfeit miracles—supernatural things. Jesus said, "Even the elect could be deceived if that were possible." What I am pointing out is this: take the kingdom of God seriously but also take the kingdom of Satan seriously. Learn to discern the ramifications of that kingdom, the power of it, the reach it has into so many lives, and realise what we are up against.

I conclude by stating quite simply that there is no question whatever which kingdom is the more powerful. I have said take Satan seriously, but never make the mistake of thinking that he can ever really challenge God's kingdom. God has given Satan an astonishing amount of rope but he will hang himself with it. God said to Satan, "You can touch Job's family. You can even touch him. You can do it. I give you permission." Poor old Job did not know what had hit him. He could not understand what was going on. It did not look as if God was in charge of his affairs when all his kids were killed in a disaster, his health went and everything was going utterly wrong. Job had to battle through to believe that God was still in control. He did not even know that God had given Satan such permission. Satan can do nothing except by God's permission, he is *under*.

As we will see, God is calling us to be a demonstration in the world that we belong to a more powerful kingdom—that is what it is all about: to dare to challenge those things of Satan. When I challenged freemasonry in Surrey I was told by the lodge that they would make my life so uncomfortable that I would have to leave, but it finished up with the grand master of the lodge renouncing it and coming to Christ. Who is more powerful? So I do not want to end this chapter on a note of being scared of Satan. No, I simply affirm: take your enemy seriously. Viscount Montgomery was never known for humility. He had many other qualities, including courage. His power to boost morale was tremendous. When he took over at El Alamein during World War II, he said, "We're going to beat Rommel" and the morale of the eighth army went up. But Montgomery never underestimated his enemy. He slept in his caravan always with a picture of Rommel, his enemy, above his bunk. When Montgomery came to speak at a school speech day in Surrey, he said to the boys, "The German soldier is the finest fighting soldier in the world, and it took someone like me to beat him." Those boys listening straightened their shoulders, lifted up their heads.

I couldn't say that; I am no match for Satan at all. He can deceive me as he can deceive you; he can twist my ideas until I am serving him even in preaching – as "an angel of light". But Christ has finished him off. Jesus gave him the fatal blow. So the last word is not with Satan.

Jesus told us to pray to the Father every day, "Your kingdom come, your will be done, on earth as it is in heaven...." But Satan managed to get the Lord's Prayer changed – did you know that? Satan had his own version of the Lord's Prayer: "Lead us not into temptation but deliver us from evil." Do you know what Jesus said when he first gave it? "Lead us not into temptation but deliver us from the evil one." Satan has managed to deceive people that evil is some*thing* rather than some*one*. So we never mention Satan in the Lord's Prayer now as Jesus intended us to. I am waiting for some church to get back to the prayer that Jesus taught us to pray. It is not the Lord's Prayer (he never prayed that prayer – he couldn't because he never had to say, "Forgive us our trespasses"). It is the Believer's Prayer. But you should finish every day praying to our Father: "Deliver us from the evil one, for yours is the kingdom, the power, the glory. Amen."

3

THE KINGDOM OF ISRAEL

Please read 1 Samuel 8.

When I want to talk about the kingdom of Israel, people say, "Well, what does that have to do with us?" A very great deal, as you will see. When Jesus came, his subject, which he preached for three solid years, was the kingdom. But he never told people what he meant by it. Have you noticed that? He described it but he never defined it. Why didn't he tell them what he meant? The answer is very simple: they all knew because he was speaking to the Jews. That was a phrase they understood perfectly well. The "kingdom of God" was something they were always talking about. Now since we very rarely hear the phrase outside church we need to retrace the history of the people of Israel to understand what is meant by it.

Teaching on this topic, I have felt the Lord has told me to put in one sentence the importance of studying the kingdom of Israel: *If we don't do better than Israel, then the same thing will happen to us that happened to them.* To expand on that: I find many Christians think that because God has taken the kingdom from Israel and given it to the church, the church cannot fail. That is dangerous complacency.

In fact, Paul writes in Romans 11: You Gentiles who now know the kingdom, don't you get conceited or arrogant or proud in your attitude to the Jews who lost it, because the same God who cut them out of the kingdom could also cut you out. They only got the kingdom by faith, and you only stand in the kingdom by faith and you could lose it just as well.

A burden I got from the Lord was that large parts of the church are going to lose the kingdom. I am sorry, but that is the truth. When the church calls itself "the new Israel" and claims to inherit all the promises of the Old Testament, but ignores all the warnings of the Old Testament, that is not fair. If you go through the Authorized Version of the Bible and look at some of the headings that are sometimes included, you will find that with everything nice that is promised to Israel in the Old Testament there is a heading: "God's love for his church." Everything nasty is headed: "God's discipline of ancient Israel". But you cannot have it both ways. If you want to claim the promises of the Old Testament then you must take the warnings with them. God will treat the new Israel in exactly the same way as he treated the old Israel. Just as he cut most of the old Israel out of the kingdom, he could cut most of a church today out of the kingdom. There is no guarantee whatever that the church building you attend is an eternal part of his kingdom.

So we are going to study the history of Israel and ask the question, "What went wrong? How did they lose the kingdom?" I shall also deal very briefly with the last question the disciples asked Jesus before he ascended to the Father: "When is Israel going to get it back?" Because just as Almighty God, King of heaven and earth, took the kingdom from Israel, he can also give it back to them and he can take it from us. So that is the seriousness. As the New Testament says, the things that were written about Israel were written that we might learn from their mistakes. The people who are not willing to learn from history are condemned to repeat the mistakes of history.

Now please read Judges 2:6–23. A generation grew up who did not acknowledge the Lord or remember the mighty things he had done for Israel. It was the problem of second-generation people of God. If you are in a new fellowship and still in the first flush of a new generation of believers, then great! Your problems will come with the second generation. How do you pass on to the next generation your living experience of the living God when they have not had that experience?

Then the Israelites did evil in the eyes of the Lord and served the Ba'als. They forsook the Lord, the God of their fathers who brought them out of Egypt. They followed and worshipped various gods of the peoples around them. They provoked the Lord to anger because they forsook him and served Ba'al and the Ashteroths. Now those two names don't mean much to you but "Ba'al" means husband and "Ashteroth" means wife. It was a pretty foul sexual religion that was in the land of Canaan. You actually went to have sex with one of the priests or the priestesses. You can imagine it was a pretty popular religion and they queued up. It was thought sexual intercourse was an act of worship – it did not matter who it was with. So you could have a different partner every time. That is what they were up against. So when we read those funny names, simply substitute in your own mind a sex-ridden society and you have got it. So it is not so very strange, even though the names are, and that is what they got into.

In his anger against Israel the Lord handed them over to raiders who plundered them. He sold them to their enemies all around whom they were no longer able to resist. Whenever Israel went out to fight, the hand of the Lord was against them to defeat them. Just as he had sworn to them, they were in great distress. Then the Lord raised up judges who saved them out of the hands of these raiders. Yet they would not listen to their judges but prostituted themselves to other gods and worshipped them. Unlike their fathers they quickly turned from the way in which their fathers had walked, the way of obedience to the Lord's commands. The Lord was very angry with Israel and said, "Because this nation has violated the covenant that I laid down for their forefathers and has not listened to me, I will no longer drive out before them any of the nations Joshua left when he died. I will use them to test Israel and see whether they will keep the way of the Lord and walk in it as their forefathers did.

The other passage, which to me is a key to understanding the history of the kingdom of Israel is 1 Samuel 8:1–9:2. (Please read it now.)

God made the world and he made people to control it. He said to man: I will be your sovereign and I will tell you what to do. You be my subjects and you can have all of this for yourself. We have seen how man rebelled against that, and Satan, waiting in the wings, stepped into centre stage and built his kingdom out of the rebellious hearts of men. So from God's point of view he had to look at planet earth and see a rival kingdom. It was not that he was helpless – he allowed it to happen. But he looked at a world that he had made very good and he saw it filled with war, disease, death, and from God's point of view he must have wondered what to do about it. What would you do in his position?

One of the things he could do would be to wipe it all out and start again. He was King and he had the power to do it. He did do that once and the account of Noah and the flood is the result. God decided to wash the whole thing out and start again, but he decided to keep just one family as the nucleus. Within hours of getting out of the ark, that family was in disgrace. The father of it was drunk and exposed himself, and the sons were taking advantage of their father's weakness. So it is a sad story and God decided not to try that way ever again – as long as the earth remained. The rest of the Bible is the story of God's plan "B" and the other way he chose to restore his kingdom on earth.

Now let me say straightaway that far too many Christians think that the only future of the kingdom lies in heaven, and that the church's job is to rescue as many individuals out of earth as we can and deliver them to heaven safely – almost as if the earth is the Titanic going down and our job is to get a few individuals into the lifeboat and deliver them to heaven safely. But the Bible says that the future of the kingdom includes the earth. It is not just getting a few more to heaven. God's objective is the re-establishment of his kingdom on earth and he has told us to pray every day that his kingdom may come on earth as it is in heaven. He is determined to have earth as well as heaven. That is why he sent Jesus to earth. Yet for all the sermons I have heard on heaven, I have not heard one on the new earth. Have you? That is as important to God as the new heaven.

After Noah's day, God resolved to establish his kingdom on earth another way, which was to start with anyone who was willing, and create a people who would be a model of his kingdom for everybody else to see and a base of operations from which he could reach the rest of the nations – not to wipe them all out, nor to try to force everybody into his kingdom, which he could have done.

Philosophers call this the scandal of particularity: why should God just start with some people instead of the others? Why should he start with the Jews instead of the Chinese? Why should he have a particular people, a chosen people? Some are offended by that. We had three children and I used to give them sweets. There were two ways in which I could do that. One was to give them each a bar — that was the way of peace! The other way was to give one of them a bag of them and say, "Share that with your brother and sister." The first way didn't test anything; the second way tested their relationships and very quickly revealed whether that day they were loving or not. If God gives something to some to share with the others, that is always a test of relationships. God did not choose to give his kingdom to the Chinese, the Indians and the Africans separately – that would not create a family. He decided to give his kingdom to a few people: the Jews—that was his way but it tests relationships. In just the same way, where some receive gifts of the Spirit, that tests the relationships within the church. People say the gifts of the Spirit divide, but they do nothing of the kind. They just reveal the divisions that already exist. If a church is not already in a relationship of love, what happens if somebody receives a special gift? Because one rejoices, others weep. But according to the New Testament, where relationships are right, if one rejoices all rejoice.

I remember a lady coming to me in our church and saying, "I really am bitter and resentful, and I'll tell you what it's about. These young people, they didn't keep the church going through all these years that we had a struggle. They march into the church, they get blessed in the Spirit, and they are speaking in tongues in weeks or days. I have been praying for years for that and I've never had it." She was very angry and she was honest enough to say, "I'm bitter."

I said to her, "But you did receive that gift."

She said, "When?"

I replied, "When they did."

"What do you mean?" she asked.

"Well they are part of your Body. If they received a gift, that means you did. So did you thank God that when they got that gift you got it? Did you say, 'thank you'?"

She said, "No."

I replied, "Well you go home and get on your knees and say, 'Lord, thank you for giving me that gift because they are part of me.'"

We are one body, not separate individuals. So she went

home and she said thank you to God – only she wasn't speaking in English when she said it!

You see, God's way is to create family, therefore he doesn't give us each something separately so we can go off into a corner and rejoice, he gives it to someone and says, "Share it with the others." I called a friend in South Africa whom I had not seen for thirty years. We had been at college together in Cambridge and his was the next study to mine. I recall that one day he came and gave me a pair of hand knitted socks. I can feel them now – lovely and warm. I said, "Thank you very much Donald, but why are you giving me this?"

"Because it's my birthday," he answered.

"Oh I'm sorry. If I had known I'd have given you something."

"No no," he said, "my mother brought us up – she was a widow, and she brought us up always to give things away on our birthday, not to receive but to give. So she sent me a dozen pairs of socks to give away to other students on my birthday."

Years later I phoned him in South Africa. I said, "Donald, this is David – David Pawson. Is your mother still alive?" He said that she was and I continued, "Will you thank her for the socks?"

He said, "Fancy your remembering."

But I could not forget. We so think that gifts are for us, and that God's way is to give me something: to give me a gift of healing so that I can be a great healer; to give me a gift of evangelism so that I can be a great evangelist. No, the only gifts he gives you are to give away to someone else.

God 's method was to give his kingdom to someone to give it away to all the others. He found an old man of eighty years of age living in a lovely home with central heating, running water in the bedrooms, and he said, "Would you be willing to live in a tent the rest of your life?" The man's name was Abraham. I am not fooling you about the comfortable house. Archaeology in Ur of the Chaldees has revealed that there was central heating in the homes and running water in the bedrooms. I showed my wife a picture of a fireplace that had been excavated there and asked her, "How do you like that?" She replied, "It's a little old-fashioned but I could live with it." I said, "It's four thousand years old." To an old man of eighty living in a comfortable home, God said, "Would you do what I tell you? Would you leave this comfortable home and would you live in a tent the rest of your life? I won't tell you where you are going to live, you just have to set off and trust me." The old man said yes. Though the whole human race were enemies of God, from that day God had one friend. That is perhaps the loveliest title that was ever given to anyone in the Bible: "Friend of God". Would God give you that title? Well, who is a friend of God? A friend of God is someone who begins by doing what God tells them – by being a subject of the King.

Now I am not going to tell you that Abraham was perfect. He lied about his wife to save his own skin. That was the result of having gone rather further than God told him to. God told him to go to Canaan so he went to Egypt. If you look on the map that is much further. Have you ever noticed how often we go much further than God tells us, once we have got on to something? You can't hold us and we go to extremes. God says, "I didn't tell you to go that far." "Oh, but Lord, that was the direction you gave us and I was off." Then there was the time that Abraham wanted to hurry God's business up for him and decided to produce a son for himself his way. He produced Ishmael.

So I am not going to tell you he was perfect, but he was a *subject*. When God said, "You go and sacrifice Isaac," he went. That was the beginning of the re-establishment of the kingdom of heaven on earth. God had one friend who would do what he told him. That is why you, if you also have the faith to be obedient to God and do what he tells you, are a son of Abraham. You are related to that eighty-year-old man. Does that get you excited or not? I hope it does. It relates you, too, to the Jews.

I want to take you on a package tour through the whole Old Testament. The person became a family; the family became a tribe; the tribe became a people; the people became slaves in Egypt. God allowed all that to happen, and it must have looked to those descendants of Abraham as if God's plan was really coming unstuck. Where was the kingdom? Where was the King? Where was the demonstration of God's sovereignty?

But God knew what he was doing. Once they had become a people, even though they were slaves God's plan was this: now I can establish my kingdom; I will demonstrate my sovereignty by getting them out of there, and I'll show them my mighty hand in doing so; then I'll tell them what it will mean to be my subjects. I'll give them a land, a place they can call their own where they can dwell in peace and prosperity, and the whole world will see what a blessing it is to live in my kingdom.

I heard a lovely story about a liberal preacher, by which I mean someone who reads his Bible with a pair of scissors in his hand. Everything supernatural gets snipped out. This preacher was preaching on the exodus from Egypt and he said, "There wasn't really a miracle then, because in fact the Red Sea at that time and place is only about eighteen inches deep and they would only need to wade across, so we mustn't think there was a miracle."

A lady in the audience shouted, "Hallelujah!"

He said, "Why did you shout, "Hallelujah?"

She replied, "the great miracle."

He said, "What great miracle?"

She said, "Drowning the Egyptian army in eighteen inches of water!"

It doesn't matter how you look at it, God's mighty arm was there. God was saying, now I'll show you who is king; it is not Pharaoh.

It seemed as if God pulled every miracle out of the bag he could: frogs, blood, boils, the lot. What he was saying was, "I'll show you my *sovereignty* first in releasing you and then I will tell you how to live in righteousness as my *subjects*."

Those are the two themes of the kingdom of God: *release* and *righteousness*. The trouble is that everybody wants release and nobody wants righteousness. People want God to be their sovereign but they are not so keen to be his subjects. The whole problem of Israel can be summed up in just that one sentence. They constantly wanted God to act sovereignly to release them but they were not willing to behave as his subjects in righteousness—that is the whole sad tale. But kingdom means sovereignty *and* subject; it means release *and* righteousness.

The kingdom of God is righteousness, not just release: "Lord, release me from my rheumatism; Lord, release me from my circumstances; Lord, release me from my overdraft at the bank; Lord, release me from my unemployment; Lord, release me." God must hear cry after cry of his people, and he has compassion. But he must wonder how many of them want to say, "Lord, release me from my sin into righteousness." I believe that is a note that he wants sounded today. Are you as anxious to be released from your bad habits as your physical sickness? That is what God is asking. Yes he wants to release you from both, but how many want to be his subjects once he has released them?

Release comes first in kingdom activity, so God said to the Hebrews in Egypt: I am going to release you; I have heard your cries and you want a release; you want to be out of that slavery; you want to be out of those depressing circumstances – then I have heard. He said, "Pharaoh, let my people go." Pharaoh said, "Who is king? I am king in Egypt. They don't go." God said, "I am king in Egypt – they do." I am not using the exact words here, I am summarising history. But who was king of Egypt? God was. He could do what he liked with old Pharaoh—even harden his heart.

So God got them out, he brought them to Sinai, and he now made clear the other side of the kingdom: I have released you; you are on your way to a land flowing with milk and honey. I can get you there in less than a fortnight; it is only eleven days from here to the land I have prepared for you. Eleven days! They could have been into God's blessing in less than a fortnight. So what went wrong that kept them forty years in the desert? There was nothing wrong with the sovereignty of the kingdom. They were not subject. This is God's eternal problem in re-establishing his kingdom on earth. He can find plenty of people who want his release but he can't find many who want his righteousness.

So what was God requiring of them? I can sum up the Ten Commandments in one word: respect. Respect is the very essence of being a subject of the kingdom: respect for God, respect for his name, respect for his day, respect for parents, respect for life, respect for property, respect for marriage, respect for reputation. That may be a strange thing to say. You may never have looked at it like that before. But the one thing that has been destroyed in our society today is respect – all those "respects" I have just mentioned. We could not be aborting a baby every six minutes if we respected life. We could not be breaking up over two marriages out of every three if we respected marriage. If shoplifting stopped tomorrow the cost of living would go down significantly, but respect for other people's goods is gone.

God asked for respect – for him and for others. Society is built on respect. When respect is destroyed, it goes. A leading comedian said some years ago that the aim of a satirical programme was to destroy respect. He said, "We intend to leave nothing sacred" – meaning nothing that people respect. So they systematically set about destroying respect for leadership, political leaders and religion and moral virtue.

Returning to our Old Testament history – God eventually brought the Hebrews into the Promised Land after forty years when they did not respect him. To keep this simple, the rest of their history can be divided into three "chapters" and we need to learn from all three. I would say that chapter one is: *before* they had kings. Chapter two: *when* they had kings; Chapter three: *after* they had kings.

We tend to think of Israel's high point as the period under their kings, particularly under King David. But in fact God's pattern of government for them was not to have their own king. The church falls into the same mistakes as Israel, again and again. We want centralised government. Now let me explain what God's intention was, how he intended to rule his people. He intended to plant them all over the land in groups, tribes, clans, and to give each of the groups their own elders, and that was all. There was to be no central government. If they got into trouble and needed serious help he would raise up what was called a "judge", a charismatic leader with gifts to get them out of that mess; to get them out of the trouble, not become a central ruler.

When Gideon got them out of trouble with the Midianites they came to him and said, "Gideon you're a great guy. Will you cover us? Will you rule over us? Will you start a dynasty? Will you be king?" Gideon knew God well. He said, "I will not be your king. I will not rule over you. You have got a king: the Lord." The substitution of human leadership for the divine kingship is a mistake that the church makes again and again. We are to have no king but Jesus. He is to rule the church, he is the only head. There are no heads in the church but Jesus. The word "head" is never applied to any church leader. We are to have local elders. From time to time God will raise up a trans-local charismatic leader for a particular purpose, but he is not to become a permanent ruler.

I am affirming things here that are pretty relevant to many of the questions being discussed today. In the days of the judges, as long as there were elders around who had personally experienced God's power, that worked all right; it was fine. But it went wrong very quickly when a new generation of elders and leaders arose who did not have personal experience of the sovereignty of God in their lives. Therefore they said, "Why be subject to him?" If you feel the next generation is not willing to be subject, then go to the root of it. Is it that they have not experienced the sovereignty?

I remember a nurse who told me that she was forced to go to church three times a Sunday. She was rebelling against it all because she did not understand what it was about. What was happening was that her parents were trying to make her a subject of the kingdom before she had experienced the sovereignty of the Lord in her life. Sometimes you have got to let your kids go and get into a mess – that they may experience the release and the sovereignty of God. If you try to make them subjects before they have experienced the sovereignty, you will produce a legalism; you will produce something that is unhealthy. I don't know whether to feel more sorry about children who are rebelling against Christian homes and getting into a mess, or children who have taken the line of least resistance and go dutifully along to church with their parents but have no personal experience of God as King. Somehow the next generation has to learn the sovereignty of God as well as being subject.

The Hebrews got into one mess after another. It says at the

end of the book of Judges: "There was no king in Israel in those days. Every man did what was right in his own eyes." Now what was wrong? The Israelite says, "What is wrong is that we have no king." God says, "What is wrong is that you each do what is right in your own eyes." Now can you see the different points of view? They said, "God, we haven't got sovereignty around. God, we want a king." God says, "No that is not the problem. I want subjects." Temptations, particularly in the sexual area, were all around the next generation and I am afraid they gave way to it. So here was a people who were not subjects of the king. God, in his sovereignty, rescued them again and again and showed that he could do it, but they blamed him for his bad government. They never thought of blaming themselves. Isn't that true? We get ourselves into a mess, and we say, "God, why did you let this happen?" It is not his fault. It is often because we were not subject to him. It was not his sovereignty that was to blame.

That was "chapter one" of the history of Israel. So finally they came to Samuel and said, "Right Samuel, things have got to change. We need a different form of government." I want to affirm this very carefully, but the answer to our situation now is not in a different form of church government. It is in a people willing to be subject. I am saying that out of the depths of my heart. There are those who say, "Well, all I need is a human king who will tell me what to do." That is not the answer; that does not produce what God wants. It can produce a subject, but what God wants is those who say, "I want to do what the King of heaven tells me." Now that does not mean that there is no room for leadership in the church. But I want to start here. The Israelites asked for a different form of government, a king. When the church copies governments of the world it is going down the wrong track. The kingdom has a very different form of government from the governments of the world. When we look at Jesus' teaching, we see what kind of government he wants. But the answer does not lie in changed human structures of government, it lies in people's hearts. Do you notice that the same book of Judges that says, "Every man did what was right in his own eyes," also says, "They all did what was evil in the sight of the Lord". That was the real problem, people saying, "Well, it's all right for me to do this," but in God's sight it was all wrong for them to do that and they were able to justify it.

If you do any counselling, you are amazed what Christians can persuade themselves is all right for Christians to do which is perfectly right in their own eyes, but in God's sight is wrong. That is the root of the problem and we keep crying out for more sovereignty, more control, more government, when really the problem is that my heart does not want to be subject to God.

So they clamoured for a human king and God said, "All right Samuel, give it to them. Let them have it." I think he meant that in more ways than one. They only had three kings as a united nation. The first turned out to be absolutely the wrong man. He looked all right but his heart was not right. He was not a subject of heaven, and a king has to be a subject of heaven. When Queen Elizabeth II was crowned in Westminster Abbey, my father had the privilege of being in the congregation for the occasion. The thing that struck him most, and that he talked about afterwards, was when she was handed a Bible and was told, "This is the royal law" – meaning: this is the law for you; this is the law to which you are to be subject. An earthly king is no use unless a subject of the King of kings. I have a picture called "King of kings". The original painting was displayed in the Royal Academy. It is the personal portrait of 159 rulers on earth. In the middle is Christ in the most luminous white robe. No artist has ever again been able to depict such a luminous robe. Behind Jesus the devil is shown, cowering away. In front of Jesus you can recognise the kings, queens and rulers. There is Napoleon folding his arms and looking at Jesus coldly from a distance. There is Edward the Confessor putting his crown down on the ground in front of Jesus. You can see the attitude of every sovereign to the King of kings in that picture. It is marvellous. You look at it and it says everything: Jesus in his majesty.

If you look at the kings of Israel and ask how many of them were subjects of the King of kings, the answer is: hardly one of them. Saul certainly wasn't – he finished up in a spiritist medium's presence playing around with occultism. But you may say, "Well, what about King David, a man after God's own heart?" Yes, there is a sense in which the nearest Israel got to the kingdom of heaven on earth was under King David, and they never forgot that. Under his leadership they came to a time of peace and prosperity that they had never known before. To this day the Jews long for that time to come back. When a Jew asks, "Will you at this time restore the kingdom to Israel?" what he means is: "Will you get us back to where David got us?"

But even King David never got fully released from the kingdom of Satan. Satan got hold of David. How? Was it through a woman, Bathsheba? I am sorry but that is the wrong answer. There is no mention of Satan whatever in that whole episode. Isn't that amazing? Do you remember I told you not to blame Satan for too much? David saw Bathsheba and broke five of the Ten Commandments in one fell swoop. I will leave you to think of which they were. He did not just commit adultery. He stole, he killed, he bore false witness. It was David's flesh which did all that. It was his own weakness. Satan did not bother him at that time. He did it all on his own and got himself in a right old mess.

So that is not what I am referring to. Only once during David's life is Satan mentioned. Satan came up to David and said, "David, how about a census? How about counting the kingdom you've got?" That was when Satan got hold of David. It was virtually the end of his career. What was wrong with it? I will explain what was wrong. You do a census for one or two reasons. You might do it out of pride to see how many people you have. It is wrong to count after your battles. You should count before your battle, but not afterwards. But it was not just pride. A census would lead to taxation and conscription. Do you know what the Lord said to David when he was going to make the census? The Lord said clearly to him: "David, are they not all your willing subjects?" Why introduce force? They all love you, they will do what you tell them. They are your willing subjects. Why start bringing the heavy hand of central government in? But I am afraid the damage was done.

Under King Solomon all the things that Samuel had warned of came true. The centralised government demanded more money, more conscripted labour and took the free sons and daughters of Israel and made them slaves of the system. If you think Solomon's reign was glory, well the Queen of Sheba thought so, but if you had asked the average Israelite, he hated it. As soon as Solomon died, civil war broke the kingdom up. What I am affirming is this: the basic problem was not the lack of sovereignty it was the lack of subjects. The people had said, "What we need is a king," but when your king is still able to be manipulated by Satan you are no better off. From then on you read the book of Kings and you find there are more bad kings than good kings.

In fact, in the northern part of the kingdom they did not have one good king, just one bad one after another who did evil in the sight of the Lord. When the people at the top of the nation do evil in the sight of the Lord, what hope is there for a nation? The rest of the people just followed, until the day came when Elijah pinpointed the problem. Elijah gathered the nation of Israel on Mount Carmel and said, "I will tell you what the root problem is. How long will you go on halting with two opinions?" Note that he did not say, "How long did you halt between them?" You may have got the impression from some preaching that here was the nation of Israel standing there thinking, "Shall we go that way? Shall we go that way? Shall we worship God or worship Baal?" But it was not: how long do you halt, stand still, wondering which way to go? That is not what Elijah said. In the Bible "halt" is not to stand still, it is to walk lame. It is an old fashioned word to us but, that is halting. Elijah was saying: "You're walking with one foot in the gutter and the other on the pavement. You're walking with one foot in Baal and the other in Yahweh. How long are you going to limp along in two kingdoms?" That is the basic thing that holds back the re-establishment of the kingdom of God on earth. It is not that the people of Israel did not want to acknowledge Yahweh, their own God, but they were playing about with other kingdoms also. So they were "halting" between the kingdom of God and the kingdom of Satan – not standing in the middle wondering which to go with, but trying to walk in both. The basic reason why the people of Israel failed to re-establish the kingdom of God on earth was that they wanted a foot in both kingdoms. They wanted a foot in the world and another foot in heaven. The basic problem in evangelism today is not how to get the church into the world but how to get the world out of the church. God is looking for people who will stop "halting" in two kingdoms, who will stop going both ways.

A friend of mine lived in Israel for forty years. He spent three days in the great hollow on the slopes of Mount Carmel, which is the only place where Elijah's challenge could have been made because there is a spring there that never runs dry, way up the mountain in this great natural arena. My friend spent three days on his hands and knees going backwards and forwards looking to see if he could find any trace of Elijah's altar – after nearly three thousand years. What faith! All he found was a little lump of rock the size of a hen's egg that had, stuck to one side of it, a sheet of what looked like green glass. But it was incredibly hard; he could not scratch the surface of this green glass, even with his wife's diamond ring. He took this piece of stone to the Geology department of the Hadassah University in Jerusalem. He said to the Professor of Geology, "What's this lump of stone?" The Professor replied, "Well you didn't find that in Israel but I'll certainly examine it and find out." The Professor said, "Do you mind if I take a slice of it off and analyse it?" My friend went back in three days and the Professor said, "You're going to be terribly disappointed. It's just a lump of limestone – just ordinary stone, but this green stuff on the side has been subject to the most indescribable heat. I can't think what sort of heat other than atomic radiation or something similar would metamorphose this stone like that." My friend knew that he had a piece of Elijah's altar. He brought that same piece of rock to the British museum, and I have seen their report on it, which was just the same: "This is an ordinary piece of stone that has completely changed its structure due to the most indescribable heat touching it."

I tell you, I could worship relics. I took one party out to Israel and I had them on their hands and knees in the same spot. I said, "Find me a piece of that stone." You know they were all looking and suddenly I saw them all stand up and walk back to me. They said, "We're not going to go on looking anymore."

I said, "Why not?"

They replied, "We realised what you'd do with it if you

had it – you would worship it. So we're not going to," and they saved me from becoming an idol worshipper! But you know, when I held that piece of stone in my hand and realised the fire of God had been on that, a shiver went up my spine. Elijah said, "I challenge you, which God is king?"

Now they have discovered through archaeology that Baal worship used to call on God to send fire. But they discovered an altar in Israel with an underground tunnel, and the priest would creep along through it. Elijah said, "Build it out in the open where we can all see. Build it right there, and I'll build mine." Elijah had the courage and the faith to laugh at them before he had proved his own. I marvel at that. He said, "Shout a bit louder. Maybe your god is on holiday. Maybe he's sitting on the toilet." Elijah said that. I know in your polite English versions it doesn't say that, it says, "He's turned aside," but that means one thing in the Middle East. He actually dared to make jokes about Baal. Then at three o'clock in the afternoon he said, "Now God, show them."

Then he ran for his life because of a woman, Jezebel. He finished up in the wilderness saying an incredible thing to God, which I am afraid I can't help laughing at. He said, "God, I'm the only subject you've got left" – and he had just run away! Does that strike you as funny? Like Simon Peter saying, "The others may run but I'm your true subject Lord." The Lord said, "Peter, before tonight's over, you'll be running too."

It is a dangerous thing to say, "God I'm the only true subject around here." Don't you ever get into that proud habit. "I'm the only keen member in our church." God very kindly didn't say, "Elijah, you're on the run so you're not my true subject." What he did say was, "Elijah, you got your sums wrong, I've got seven thousand." I heard an Arab preacher in Jerusalem begin his sermon like this, "Why did Elijah have a nervous breakdown? Because he didn't have any fellowship with the seven thousand." That is quite an introduction!

Have you noticed that God did not say, "There are seven thousand who have remained true to me," he said, "I have reserved seven thousand." It was God's sovereignty that had done it. God was saying: "I've kept seven thousand for myself." That is to be the story of the rest of Israel's history – that God has always kept a remnant. Even to this day there has never been a single period in the last three thousand years when there haven't been some of Israel who were true subjects of the kingdom of heaven. It is an amazing thing. The church didn't replace the Jews; the Gentiles were grafted in among the branches that remained. There have always been Jews who were true to the King. For the last two thousand years, there has always been a remnant of Jews who believed that Jesus was the Messiah. Did you know that?

Ultimately they became such bad subjects of the king that the prophets were sent to tell them, "Out of this land. Out of God's sight. Go back to slavery," and they went to Babylon. You might have said, "God, that was a failure, wasn't it? You didn't get your kingdom established, did you, through those people? You had better try someone else." I marvel at God, who says: no, I'll bring them back and we'll start again. If God wiped his hands of people the first time they failed him, I would not be preaching. What a king to have, who says, "I don't let go that easily." In fact, the reason why there is such a nation as Israel on the map today is very simple: God says, "I hate divorce"; he hates breaking faith once he has made a promise.

So God brought them back but he never gave them a king again. They had a temple again but not a palace. They had priests again, but no kings. What many people do not realise is that for most of their history the people of Israel did not have kings. I know we read the Bible and the book of Kings and think they must have had king after king after king, but in fact it was a very brief period when they had kings. The kingdom was really to be established in such a way that the King was in heaven, not on earth.

God had a beautiful one up his sleeve and I find myself chuckling when I think of this: God's ideal is to bring them back to a view of the kingdom on earth where the king is in heaven. This is what he thought up: I'll give them a Son of David and I'll send him to earth, and then I'll bring him back to heaven to reign. Isn't that simple? He took their hopes and somehow transformed them. They just wanted to return to the time of David with an earthly king, with the peace and prosperity of that time, and God was not doing that. He would give a Son of David who would bring the kingdom back here. He will reign from heaven, and there would be a people on earth whose king is in heaven. That is God's objective, that is the model on earth that he is looking for in the church, too: to have a people on earth with no visible king, no centralised government, but a people who are so subject to the king of heaven that they operate together in harmony.

What sort of unity would most impress our nation? Every denomination getting into one denomination and having one huge headquarters in the capital? No, what would impress them would be to find in every corner of the country people thinking the same way, doing the same thing, enjoying the same joy, enjoying the same peace. People would scratch their heads and say, "How come you go to Land's End or John O' Groats and you find the same thing happening? They don't have any centralised government and they don't have anybody telling them what to do. Who is organising it? Who is controlling it? Well, these are subjects of the King of heaven." We still think the answer is structural government and all coming under the same guy, and all coming under the same denomination. That is not God's way. His way is to have people living all over the place with their own elders, but obeying the King of heaven and doing what is right in his eyes. Then you will see a unity among God's people right the way through, and it will work. We crave for earthly government to put us right, and God's way is: be subject to the King.

Was the kingdom of Israel a failure or a success? For most of the Israelites it was a failure. They were not subjects of the King. They had experienced his sovereignty again and again, but God did not experience their subjection. They were not subject to him, so was it a failure? No. There was always, all the way through, a remnant of true Jews who were subjects of the kingdom. When Jesus was born there were a couple mentioned there: Simeon and Anna. They were subjects of the kingdom. They were looking for the kingdom. Their heart's desire was to see God's King come. Simeon was able to say, "Lord, let your servant go in peace now. I don't mind dying now," and all he had seen was a baby – but he was looking.

The remnant clung to two promises of God. One was that he would send them a King of his choosing, who would establish his rule on the earth, not just for Israel but for all the nations. So there was to be a national restoration of the kingdom, but it was also to be international. The prophet Isaiah had said, "It is too small a thing for God to restore Israel. You are to be a light to the Gentiles." God was thinking of the international scene.

Modern Israel still does not see the kingdom. Some Jews and an increasing number of Israelis do. There are many indigenous fellowships of Israeli believers in Jesus now in Israel. It is a miracle. Instead of all these dreadful denominational buildings going up in Jerusalem, and everybody importing all their own traditions into that place, there are indigenous Israeli fellowships who believe in *Yeshua HaMaschia* (Jesus the Messiah), there in Israel. God has kept that remnant and we Gentiles must never forget that the kingdom is Jewish – "salvation is of the Jews".

So the Old Testament closes with tremendous hope, waiting for a King to come who would establish the kingdom. Now those who hoped for the king were divided clearly into two groups. Jesus had problems with this when he came. One group could only see the national kingdom, but the other group could see the international. Some could only see the restoration of a Davidic kingdom, but others were longing for the kingdom of God, when God would reign on the earth. They were longing for the day when the house of the Lord would be established in the mountain of the Lord and the nations would disarm and learn war no more. Disarmament won't come until the kingdom of God comes. Under his rule of righteousness the nations will be able to disarm; international disputes will be settled by the King.

So there was the Jewish hope for a simple national restoration, which asked: when are you going to restore the kingdom to Israel? But there was also the international hope that would say: I am looking for the kingdom of God on earth. The rabbis who looked for the kingdom used to say, "A prayer is not a prayer that does not ask for the kingdom." That is quite a statement. There are rabbis in Jerusalem today who would say, "Your prayer is not a prayer if you did not include within it a prayer, 'Your kingdom come.'" Jesus said, "You pray every day, 'Your kingdom come...'." We are going to see the exciting news that when Jesus was born the kingdom had come.

4

THE KINGDOM OF CHRIST

Please read Isaiah 9:1–7;
Matthew 3:1–12; 4:12–17; 5:1–10; 6:7–10; 6:31–33;
13:31–52.

To "bring out of the store room new treasures as well as old" is what I hope to do in this section of our study. Jesus is virtually saying in Matthew 13:52 that if you understand the New Testament, you will also understand the Old, and you will be able to bring the Old and the New together. If you have been instructed in the old way of the law and the new way of the kingdom, you can see the purpose of the whole.

In this book so far, we have considered the kingdom of God, the kingdom of Satan and the kingdom of Israel – and that is all in the Old Testament. Now we are at something of a watershed. We are moving into the New, but we are able to bring things new and old out of our treasure. We are able to see the Old and the New Testament together as the single narrative of God's re-establishment of his kingdom on earth.

We recall that the Jews were left looking forward to a day when God in his sovereignty and power would re-establish his rule on earth. They believed he would do it primarily with the nation of Israel and from there would spread his rule to the nations, to the ends of the earth. I am rather excited whenever I read in the Old Testament of the distant isles, because that refers to the British Isles. It really does! In those days, in the days of Abraham in fact, they used to send to Cornwall for tin. The Phoenicians knew about these islands, and when you talked about the most distant parts of the world in those days, you talked about the distant isles – the furthest the sailors went, which was here.

I am not a British Israelite, but I am just excited whenever I read in the book of Isaiah that it will be told in the distant isles—that is coming true today. God's hope for the future was his promise that he would establish his rule on earth not just in Israel, but to the distant isles, to the ends of the earth. So to the Jews, the phrase "the kingdom of God" meant the day when God would re-establish his rule on earth everywhere, and they believed also from what the prophets had told them that he would do it through a king, a descendant of David, of God's choice—an even greater king than David. That was the heart of the Jewish hope. Those who knew their scriptures well, also knew that God had made certain promises about the subject side of the kingdom as well as about the sovereign side but, conveniently, most of them overlooked that.

The root of the problem was not that God wasn't acting in sovereignty, but that his people would not be his subjects and I want to tell you this: it is hypocrisy to pray for revival, saying, "God, come and take over this land. Lay bare your mighty arm, we've prayed and prayed," if you are not at the same time willing to be his subject.

It was that kind of hypocrisy that the prophets laid bare, but the big difference between the Old and the New Testaments is summed up very simply in this way. In the Old Testament God was saying: I will exercise my sovereignty and release you, but will you live righteously? In other words, in the Old Testament the kingdom was made up of an offer and a demand. God offered release, but demanded righteousness in response. The New Testament does not do that. In a word, the New Testament offers release *and* offers righteousness. God promised not only to help them on the sovereignty side, but to help them on the subject side. Isn't that beautiful of God?

So he was virtually saying: I realise the problem is your subjection. You can't make it, you can't keep the laws, and you can't keep the covenant. So the prophets said God was going to make not only an act of sovereignty to restore his kingdom, but he was going to help subjects to be subjects in two ways. First, by forgiving their sins and, second, by pouring out his Spirit. Frankly, you will never be a subject of the King without first experiencing the forgiveness of your sins, and then having the Holy Spirit poured out on you. Isn't it beautiful that righteousness is no longer a *demand*? That also is now an *offer*.

So the prophets said: In the last days I will make a new covenant with you. I'll forgive your sins and I'll write my laws not outside you, but inside you, so that you'll want to keep them. What an offer! Even in the Old Testament days there were some – Abraham was one, David was another – who realised something of this. In fact, David's prayer after he had messed around with Bathsheba is remarkable. He said, "Lord, I was conceived in sin, I'll never make it. Renew a right spirit within me, create a new heart in here. Do something—don't take your Holy Spirit away." So even in the Old Testament there were those who realised that righteousness is not what God *demands* from you, but what he *offers to give you*—that is good news. The Mosaic covenant was bad news. The Mosaic covenant was: I'll release you provided you keep all the commandments and produce righteousness. It's a cul-de-sac, a non-starter. The good news of the New Testament is that God says he will not only be your sovereign, but will also be the subject in you.

That was the start of the Reformation. Martin Luther was trying to be righteous before God, and he meant business. He would flog himself until he fell unconscious in his monastery cell, to try and get sins out of himself. In a thunderstorm he fell on the ground in terror of a God who might strike him dead, and he knew that he had not produced righteousness to get by the Day of Judgment. Luther searched the Bible, and every time he read the word "righteousness" he cringed. It was a horrible word to him because it stood for a level of right living that he could not get up to. Then one day, like a flash of illumination, he realised that the phrase "the righteousness of God" means what it says and that God says: I've got enough righteousness for myself and for you. When he realised that God was not only willing to be his sovereign and release him, but also willing to be in him the subject and give him his divine righteousness, he was free and the Reformation began.

You will never make it – you will never be good enough. The good news of the kingdom in the New Testament is "I've got enough righteousness for you as well as me." That explains why it was prostitutes who got into the kingdom first in Jesus' day. It also explains why the religious people did not get in, because they were still trying to be righteous. I hope you are getting excited in your heart as you read this. I am touching something very fundamental. The Old Testament did not work because the people could not make themselves subjects and they wanted the sovereignty.

Now the key to understanding the ministry of Jesus is that his primary concern was to get subjects for the kingdom, not to establish the sovereignty. You will only understand the conflicts that he went through and the reason they put him on the cross if you realise that the crowd wanted him to be king, whereas he was wanting them to be his subjects. He wanted not only to release them from the kingdom of Satan; he wanted to give them righteousness. It was only the bad people who realised that what they thought was a hopeless situation was in fact the very doorstep into the kingdom. It was the irreligious people, who had given up trying to be righteous, who discovered the kingdom of God.

When Jesus was born, a lot of royal language was used. "Where is he who is born king of the Jews?" Now there were very few who could see beyond Israel. Most of them were looking for a king of the Jews, and that was because for five or six hundred years, Israel had been slaves – not in Egypt or Babylon, but in their own country, they had been under the heel of the Persians, the Egyptians, the Syrians, the Greeks and the Romans. Only for a few years, under a family of Jews called the Maccabees, did they have a measure of political freedom, but it quickly disappeared. For those five or six centuries, they were under an enemy authority in their own land, never mind Egypt or Babylon. They naturally longed for someone to release them in their own land and they were looking for a king of the Jews.

Furthermore, for four hundred years, God had not said a word to them. It was a long time to be out of touch. In that period there was no prophet. Nobody said, "Thus says the Lord," and that is why there is a gap of four hundred years between the Old and the New Testaments. There were books written in that period which we call the Apocrypha, but they should not be in your Bible because, while they are interesting, there is no word from God in them.

Do you know what happens when people don't hear from God directly? They get into theological argument about the Bible. You get scribes—they have no immediate word from God, so they have to pick and pick in the written word of God and they finish up in liberal and conservative theological schools. That is what happened. They called themselves Pharisees and Sadducees. I tried to remember these two at school, and I could remember the Sadducees easily enough because they didn't believe in an afterlife and so they were "sad, you see" and I could always remember that. Then I remembered the Pharisees because they did believe in an afterlife and so I used to say, "Far, I see," and that reminded to me what they were!

They split up into different theological groups because they had not heard from God; when you hear the living word from God, you can't spend a lot of time in theological argument, picking and nitpicking at text. So they had the Bible, they had the words of God in the past, but they had no word of God in the present. Then, suddenly, it went round Israel like a prairie fire: the rumour. "Have you heard? There's a prophet again!" When you have waited four hundred years to hear from someone, that is exciting news, and people said, "Where is he?" "He's down by the Jordan River, and he dresses just like Elijah used to."

Can you imagine the wave of excitement? When you've been waiting for God to say and do something for centuries; when grandparents would take their grandchildren on their knee and say, "One day, God will speak again; one day, he will send a king and he will release us from all our troubles," and the voice of God was heard again, they went to him from every quarter to hear what John was saying from God. He said, "Get baptised," and it caused the same controversy then that it causes now. Why? Because no Jew had ever been baptised; it was all right for Gentiles, but not for Jews. "We are in the covenant people – we belong. My parents were Jews; my grandparents were Jews. I'm in; I was born into it." John the Baptist's message was: Don't you dare think you belong because your parents belonged. The kingdom's very near, so you had better get cleaned up. You had better have a bath. You had better confess what is dirty in your life and get it cleaned out because the kingdom is coming and when the kingdom gets established, everything dirty is going to go.

Isn't it interesting? We always want God to clean every-body else up. "God, will you come and put *them* right and will you come and stop *them* doing that?" We want God to clean the place up, but not *me*. John the Baptist knew where the kingdom would begin. It would begin when somebody said, "I want my life cleaned up."

I know of a young man who was a Hell's Angel and as far from God as you can get. He was into everything, and then he became a Christian. Christ straightened his life up, and he wanted to be baptised. In fact, he knew that God was telling him to be to wash away his past. He did not want to be seen being baptised though, because he was covered in tattoos from his waist to his neck. He noticed that when you went into water your shirt went transparent and church people did not seem to go in for tattoos. So he was a bit embarrassed, but he was more than embarrassed about one of the tattoos. When he was a Hell's Angel, he had had the devil tattooed on his body. There was Satan for all to see on his body and he thought, "How can I be baptised and let them see that?"

So he went to a plastic surgeon and said, "Could you do anything about this?" The surgeon said, "Not on the National Health Service, that's cosmetic surgery, but I could try and do a skin graft – though it will cost you a lot of money and take a lot of time." This lad thought, "Well, I don't have the money and I want to get on with it." So he decided to be embarrassed and he asked for baptism. He went down into the water to wash away and bury his past, and when he came up out of the water one of the tattoos had gone – just one! The devil was washed off his body in the water of baptism. That is what baptism is meant to be. It is a sign of the kingdom; it is to wash away your past. It is to say, "I'm making a clean start. I want to be clean because the kingdom is going to be a clean place, and I want to get cleaned up before the kingdom comes."

So the message of John the Baptist was that you had better repent: those of you who have got too many clothes, go and get rid of some, give them to the poor; those of you fiddling your accounts, go and get your finances straight; those of you who have been bullying others, you had better stop fighting. He was a very practical preacher. Some people like "nice" gospel sermons that never touch anything, but John the Baptist touched things. He said to the king of the country, "You shouldn't have that woman as your wife, it's not legal." According to Jesus' teaching, those who remarry a divorcee are living in adultery. Where are the Christians who are prepared to get up and say that? John the Baptist was fearless in putting his finger on things that would not match up with the kingdom. He would say: "You'd better get cleaned up."

It is interesting that John did not heal anybody. Not a single miracle happened in his ministry—no signs, no wonders, just the word of God. He was an amazing man and he paid for it with his life. He had lived a lonely life. He had been out in the desert with God ever since he was a boy, and God had said, "John, the King is coming." It was the custom in those days, as it still is, that if royalty is visiting or coming to a place, someone is sent before, to get the place ready. If the Queen is going to come to your city, I will guarantee there will be somebody from Buckingham Palace months earlier to say, "Get ready, the Queen's coming! Buy a red carpet, clean up that rubbish!"

John the Baptist was the one who had to come and say, "Prepare the way of the Lord. Fill up the valleys, reduce the mountains; get a decent road straight so that he can ride in." The King came, and it was Jesus. His message was exactly the same as John's: Repent, for the kingdom is here; it is right among you now. If you study carefully, the implication is very clear. Jesus was saying: I am the kingdom. He said the same things about himself and about the kingdom, so that they were synonyms – interchangeable terms. That is a remarkable thing to say, and you can imagine the excitement at the beginning of his ministry at the announcement: the kingdom of God has arrived.

Now we want to look at the implications of that, because his congregation went down from five thousand to twelve overnight. He began with a huge following and it dwindled until he finally said to the few that were left, "Are you going to leave me too?" Peter said no – what Jesus said was what they had been waiting to hear. Now the puzzle is this: why did Jesus become so unpopular when at the beginning he did not even need to book a hall? He did not need a publicity agent! Just the fact that he was in town was enough to pack the streets with people who wanted to meet him and hear him. The reason is, very simply, that he refused to concentrate on the *sovereignty* of the kingdom, but he went hard after finding *subjects* and that was not so spectacular.

Now let us look first at the sovereignty that he did bring. I am amazed that there was never a situation in which Jesus was at a loss or out of control. It did not matter whether it was a mad demoniac or a storm on the Sea of Galilee, or five thousand people with nothing to eat, there was never a situation in which he was not in total control. Even when they tried to throw him off the cliff at Nazareth, he was in total control. You could see the sovereignty of the kingdom in Jesus. He was King of every situation. If he met a funeral in the road, he would tell the corpse to get out of the coffin. He was King of disease, King of death, King of nature, King of everything. So much so that when they saw what sovereignty he had over every human need, over every human circumstance, over everything, they said, "We want to make you king." They offered him the throne within about six months of his beginning his ministry, and he refused it. They believed this was what they had been waiting for: you are the king, and we are prepared to march behind you, drive the Romans out, set up a throne in Jerusalem and put a crown on your head; we want you as our king! As the people wanted King David, we want you. Jesus refused it. Time and again they recognised his sovereignty and wanted to have it publicly displayed, but every time he said no. Do you know the reason? Because he knew what was in man and he wouldn't trust any man – we are told that – because he knew that none of them as yet were his subjects. That is what he was after. You will find that where they wanted him to heal, he wanted to preach. One morning, in the house in Capernaum where Jesus and his disciples were staying, his bed was empty and they could not find him anywhere. But when they opened the front door, the main street was jammed from end to end with sick people wanting healing. I used to wonder why there were so many sick people in Capernaum. I now know—just down the road was the health spa, the "Harrogate of Galilee", Tiberias. To this day, Jewish people and Gentiles from all over the world come to Tiberias to bathe in the waters to try to heal their rheumatism. Crippled people come to the hot springs. So when people heard that there was a healer just a mile or two up the road at Capernaum, they left the hot springs and Capernaum was crowded.

But where was Jesus? We have got a revival on our hands! Look at the crowds wanting to be healed! They found Jesus in the hills behind Capernaum, and when they asked what he was doing there, he told them he had gone to pray. Everybody was looking for him, but Jesus said that he was going to the next town to preach. Did you ever notice that?

Even when he healed people and got them released from their disease, they refused to become his subjects. Here is one example. He met a man with leprosy, an outcast from his society. Because of his physical disease, he could not even go to his own family – and Jesus touched him. I was taken to a hospital for lepers once and I had to force myself to touch them. I confess I could only do it (this is many years ago) because I had to keep reminding myself: Jesus did. There is a human revulsion. Jesus touched him and released him from leprosy. Then Jesus wanted the man to be his subject, giving him his first two orders as the healed man's King: "Don't tell anyone," and, "Go and show the priest." Do you know what the next verse in the Bible is? "So the man went out and told everyone everywhere that Jesus had cured his leprosy." Are you getting the message? People were healed from all manner of disease; they were set free from demons – but Jesus could not find anyone to be his subject. Who would obey his orders? Think of the climax of his ministry, when he took the disciples up to the amazing place where the Jordan comes out of Mount Hermon. It is strange – there is a rock wall and then the river just comes out, forty feet wide! It comes down inside the mountain from the melted snow, and then out of a rock wall, from an underwater crack. It has been a place of religion and superstition for millennia. Carved in the rock wall are niches where they put all sorts of gods. There was the god Pan, said in mythology to have appeared in the form of a man. There was Caesar, who was a man who claimed to be god, and all these god-men and man-gods were in the niches there when Jesus took his disciples. What a place to take them! As they looked at these statues of god-men and man-gods, Jesus said, "Who do men think I am?" They said, "Men think you are a reincarnation of some great man from the past—Jeremiah, Elijah, John the Baptist."

"And who do you think I am?"

Peter said, "You are the Christ."

Now to us the word "Christ" is a religious word, so let me translate it: "You are God's anointed King". Peter was saying that he recognised. He was the first man to say it. Demons had said it before, but Peter was the first human to recognise. "You are the Christ; you are the King."

Jesus said that was right: it was my Father who helped you to that conclusion, Peter, and that is the truth. Now, Peter, the next step is for us to go to Jerusalem and for me to be crucified.

"Oh no, you're not doing that!"

Can you see that Peter even recognises the King, but will not be subject? He will argue, he will rebel, he will say no, I know better than you – and, to the last day before Jesus died, Peter was telling Jesus what to do. Jesus said, "I want to wash your feet, Peter."

"You're not going to do that Lord, I'm sorry, no."

He calls him "Lord" but he won't let him do it. That is hypocrisy again, and Jesus said, "Peter, if I don't wash your feet we can't be friends."

"Oh well in that case, here, wash my hands, my head."

"Peter, I just said your feet."

Do you realise that right up to the moment Jesus died he had not found one subject for the kingdom? He had released many, he had exercised the sovereignty of the kingdom in many lives, but he had not found one who was utterly loyal to him. Even his nearest friends ran away and Peter, who said, "Well, the others may let you down but I won't, Lord," swore to a little servant girl that he had never met Jesus.

So there is a sense in which the Lord's earthly ministry for three years was apparently a failure. In fact, on the day of his crucifixion it looked an utter disaster. Here was the King, who had come to re-establish the rule of God on earth; he is left without a single subject, and he is dead. Yet, you know, something had got through. Even a dying thief said to Jesus that he believed Jesus was the King and would get his kingdom. Could he have a place in it? There was that strange quirk of Pilate's flickering defiance at the end, when he put a little notice above the dying Jesus: This is the King of the Jews. A Roman centurion had recognised Jesus' sovereignty and said, "You've only got to say the word, and my servant will be healed. I recognise authority when I come up against it."

Now let me backtrack a little. The Jews expected God's kingdom to come on a national and an international scale, and they were puzzled because Jesus did not seem interested in either. He neither seemed to want to set himself up as king of the Jews, nor when the Greeks made an offer to have him, was he interested in them either. The Greeks were sort of saying to Jesus: the Jews may not want you, but come over and minister among us; we will welcome you. But he would not go there – he concentrated on the kingdom as an individual thing first.

Have you ever noticed that whenever he talked about the kingdom, he talked in terms of individuals? "The kingdom of heaven is like *a man* looking for treasure" – or like *a woman* hiding yeast. It is almost as if Jesus was declaring: I will establish the kingdom of God nationally and internationally, but the way I begin is with individuals; I cannot build a national and international kingdom unless I have individual subjects who are subject to the King. So, very early on, he gathered his followers to him, took them up the mountain and taught them what it is to be a subject in the kingdom: "Blessed are the poor in spirit, for theirs is the kingdom of heaven" – and that was how he began.

He taught that if you are going to be a subject in the kingdom, there is to be no anger in your life at all. He said, "You've heard it said 'you shall not kill,' but I say...." That is the King making his laws. You must not even have contempt in your heart for anybody else. You mustn't call them a fool, because to be angry with someone or to despise them is to be in danger of hellfire – that is not kingdom living. "You've heard it said, 'Don't commit adultery'...." Jesus taught that you may never have climbed into a bed with someone else's wife, but if you have looked at a girl and wondered what it would be like to have her in bed, you are not fit to be a subject in my kingdom. He was very strict on divorce – far stricter than almost every denomination today. (See my book *Remarriage is Adultery, Unless....*)

He lifted the standards of the kingdom far higher than Moses ever did. Now here is one that's going to get you if I haven't touched anything already. Subjects of the kingdom are not allowed to worry. Did you know that Jesus said more about worry in the Sermon on the Mount than about adultery? But when did a church last discipline a member for worrying? Worry is a libel on your heavenly Father. You are saying, if you worry, that your Father cares more about his garden and his pets than he does about his children – because he feeds the birds of the air and he looks after the flowers of the field, and therefore if you are worried you are saying, "My Father doesn't care".

I never knew our three children to worry about the next meal, because whenever they came in there was a meal for them. Imagine if I or my wife had heard a neighbour say, "Your children were telling me they're really worried as to whether they'll get any food tomorrow." How do you think we would have felt if others were talking about our children like that? Jesus taught that a subject of the kingdom trusts. The best welfare state you could ever belong to is the kingdom of heaven. You seek first his kingdom and his righteousness and everything else is thrown in as a bonus. You will always have enough to wear. You will have enough to eat. The bills will be paid if you are a subject of the kingdom.

When you read through the Sermon on the Mount, you think, "That's impossible – I'll never be a subject of the kingdom," but Jesus refused to lower his standards one inch.

In fact, he pushed them sky high – literally, heaven high. Then you find that in the last six months of his ministry he hardly healed anybody. He just laid it on thick: no man is worthy of the kingdom if he puts his hand to the plough and looks back; unless you prepare to give everything you have got – no use in the kingdom. He seems to have spent his time putting off the people who did follow him: why are you following me? Are you prepared to take up a cross and die on it? Okay, you can come. That is not the way to win friends and influence people! Jesus was determined to get subjects for the kingdom, but the amazing thing to me is the people who did follow him, even though he raised the standards so high. Why? Because they felt instinctively that even though he set such high standards, he could help them to reach them. He said, "My burden's light. My yoke's easy." Fancy saying that after preaching the Sermon on the Mount! But do you realise the significance of the expression "my yoke"? A yoke is a piece of wood with two notches in it and it links two animals which then pull together. When Jesus said, "Take my yoke upon you," he is not saying take the Sermon on the Mount and try to live up to it, he is saying: here, get under the other end of this with me and we will pull together and we will make it.

So when a woman taken in adultery looked in Jesus' face and he said, "Go and sin no more," she began to believe she could. I am amazed that Jesus had the capacity to teach the highest moral standards that anyone has ever taught and yet be a friend of sinners. Usually, when Christians moralise they put sinners off. He had the capacity of saying that is the standard, but come to me all you who labour and are heavy laden – those of you who can't make it.

I wonder whether you realise what the word "sinner" means in the New Testament. It doesn't mean cannibal, it doesn't mean criminal. I used to love taking groups out to

Israel and introducing them to the land. Some people said, "We love to go with you to Israel. We learn far more from you there than we do when you preach in church." I said to one, "Why?" They said, "Because you're just talking all the time and it's natural to be talking as you are on the way." Most of Jesus' teaching was not in a pulpit. It was while they walked along the road – and one person who came with me recorded some fourteen hours of my comments on the bus. It seems natural to point and say, "Look there are some sheep and some goats; watch what that shepherd does with them." I remember being on a bus on one trip, and there was an Israeli guide and an Israeli driver. From the front, through the microphone, I said, "Now I think it's time I told you what a 'sinner' was, otherwise you might not understand." We had just been through the Mea Shearim, the very Orthodox quarter of Jerusalem where you get the Jews with ringlets and long coats and notices about women's dress and all the rest. I then said, "I want you to realise what a sinner is. When you read the word 'sinner' in the Gospels, I want you to think of our driver and our guide, because they are sinners." They sort of stiffened up and looked away. I explained, "A sinner in the Bible days was not a very bad person, but someone who had given up on religion because they just couldn't make it. It was too heavy, and technically the word 'sinner' was for someone who did not try to keep all the Sabbath laws – ordinary people who said, 'I just can't cope with religion; it's just too much,' and got on with the business of daily living." Now I knew the driver and I knew the guide, and that they were not Orthodox, not religious. They had given up trying. It was too heavy. I said, "Do you realise that if Jesus was right here today in the flesh, it is our driver and our guide he would be making friends with, not the people you have just seen in the Mea Shearim who are desperately trying to keep the law?" It was the first time the driver and the guide had heard that Jesus was the kind of person who liked people who had given up on religion because it was too heavy.

Back home, I had a burden from the Lord which I believe was prophetic when visiting another part of the UK – that when God moves in sovereignty in that place he is going to bypass the religious people. Religion is offensive to God, and in that area there was far too much religion. You had better get your life cleaned out of religion if the kingdom is coming. I believe he is going to touch irreligious people – people right outside.

I had the privilege of listening to a glorious testimony from a woman who was a prostitute in Aberdeen and who relieved the oilmen of their money when they came off the oil rigs. She had a bedroom which she wanted to be the finest bedroom in Aberdeen. She wanted the walls in black and the ceiling all mirror, and a big bed. She got the money for that bedroom in which to entertain the men, then one day she finished up in the mental hospital, and her basic problem was simply that men used her. They didn't love her; she felt no one loved her. Then one day she met Jesus in the streets of Aberdeen. I tell you, she's now a princess, a lovely person. She's beautiful. Of that bedroom (which has not quite the same decoration now!) she said, "Jesus, from now on this bedroom is for you only." It's the King's room.

I tell you there is more joy in heaven over that girl in Aberdeen than over all the religious ladies with their tight lips singing the metrical psalms on Sunday. Do you believe that? The kingdom welcomes the irreligious. Jesus had big problems with religious people who were trying to work their passage and trying to be righteous. The most you can achieve of your own righteousness is you can get the outside right. You can manage respectability, but you can't manage righteousness. Although you can get the outside right, you can never get the inside right. You can even sit at Holy Communion and have the most terrible thoughts inside and nobody else knows. You look very respectable; nicely dressed.

Such religiosity is the enemy of the kingdom of God and Jesus would call it today what he called it then – "whitewashed sepulchres" – because I know also of a prostitute who went looking for Christ in church and finished up in an elder's bed. Forgive me for being blunt, but Jesus was blunt and he called things by their real name. He wanted reality and he would rather have a crooked tax collector and a prostitute in his kingdom than religious people, and they would rather have it too. It says, "They seized the kingdom violently" – they snatched at it as if it was their only lifeline. At last they had met somebody who gave them some hope of ever getting out of the mess they were in.

Now all this was very surprising to the Jewish people. It was a surprise to the religious leaders that he mixed with people like that. It was a surprise to the common people that he would not be king when they wanted him to be king. But what was he after? He was after releasing people from the kingdom of Satan and helping them to be subjects of the kingdom of heaven. Yet, as I have pointed out, it would look as if by the time he came to die, he had not got one. There were people who had been raised from the dead. There were people who had been healed of leprosy. There were people out of whom legions of demons had been cast, yet when the crunch came, only one person went to Calvary – alone. On the day that Jesus died, the kingdom of heaven on earth was reduced to one person. You see, not only was Jesus the perfect sovereign of the kingdom in total control and power over every conceivable situation, but he was also the perfect subject of the kingdom. He was the first person who throughout his lifetime had been subject to the will of

God perfectly. When he finally struggled in the garden of Gethsemane with the last call of duty where the Father had told him to go to the cross, he sweated blood.

Never think it was easy for Jesus to be sinless. He learned obedience through the things he suffered, and he agonised: Father, is there no other way? But there would have been no subjects of the kingdom unless Jesus went this way. It was the only way to set people totally free from Satan. Jesus had to break the power of the prince of this world. Jesus finally said to the Father, "Not my will, but yours be done." He became obedient to death at the age of thirty-three when every instinct in us is would have held on to life.

On the day that Jesus was hanging on a cross, people were saying: save yourself; get yourself out of the trouble; you've saved everybody else; you've proved yourself King in every other situation – prove it now, that you are the King of the Jews; get off the cross. He could have done it easily, but his Father had said stay, and he stayed.

That day, Satan's power was smashed. That day the kingdom of Satan suffered a mortal blow. A human being had stayed out of his kingdom for his whole life and there was a foothold on earth in the human race for the kingdom of heaven on earth. It is true that Jesus died in our place and that he was punished for our sins – but I think the deepest meaning of the cross is this: that day he triumphed over principalities and powers and made a show of them openly. He broke the power of the prince of this world.

It is true that wherever the message of the cross has been preached, Satan's power has been smashed and people have been released. The blood of Jesus is more powerful than anything Satan can do. You can deliver people from Satan and from his demonic powers through that one day's act. But I say again, the kingdom of heaven on earth was represented that day in one man only – Jesus, but he won. "It's finished.

It's completed. I've done it." From then on the kingdom could be re-established and subjects could be set free from Satan – forgiven, released.

One of the things that Satan uses most perhaps to keep hold of people is guilt – that strange mixture of fear and shame which dares not bring something out into the open, and it is the hidden things in our lives that Satan uses to keep us chained, isn't it? But Jesus died in the darkness so that these things could be brought into the light and smashed. The cross finally established the kingdom on earth and the kingdom has never looked back since. It may have seemed a bit like a grain of mustard seed. To the Roman authorities it was just one among thousands of crucifixions somewhere out at the edge of the empire, but to the universe it was the longest day – the turning point.

After he had risen from the dead, Jesus spent time talking to his disciples. What about? He had only one subject for six whole weeks. They went to Bible school for that period. It was the first time he had given them any Bible study, but he took them through every part of the scriptures – the law, the prophets, the psalms. What was his theme? Very simple – the kingdom of God. If you read the opening verses of Acts, it says that for those six weeks he appeared alive to them – he proved that he was alive with many infallible proofs. They knew he was alive. They knew he had conquered even death itself, but it says he instructed them concerning the kingdom of God. Then he took them out to the Mount of Olives and they realised it was goodbye. They knew something was ending.

Now if you had the chance to ask Jesus one question only, personally, what would you ask him? It is very interesting. The disciples had walked with him for three years; they had listened to him giving them instruction for six weeks on the kingdom of God. It must have been marvellous to have Jesus' interpretation. There was just one thing the disciples still did not understand: they expect the kingdom to be established nationally; they believe he is the King of the Jews, then why didn't he get on with restoring the kingdom to Israel?

A common Christian answer, throughout the Christian world, is unfortunately this: that is a silly question; Jesus was finished with Israel; Israel had failed, and the kingdom will be taken from this nation and given to a nation that produces fruits worthy of it. So the common conception is that the kingdom of God now has nothing to do with the Jews and nothing to do with Israel. It has been handed over to the church. Don't fall for that one! Whenever a question is asked, you should always listen to the underlying premises. Hidden in every question are certain assumptions, and if those assumptions are wrong, you should not answer the question. For example, if you ask me have I stopped beating my wife, that is a loaded question; there is a premise in it. There is an assumption in it and I would not answer the question with a "yes" or "no" because either way I would be acknowledging your assumption that I once did. So, for example, if the disciples had said, "Jesus, are you going to assassinate Pontius Pilate now?" and he had replied, "It's not for you to know when" – what would you judge from that? You might think that the question was a valid one. Now, when they said, "Will you at this time restore the kingdom to Israel?" there were four assumptions in the question. First assumption: that Israel once had the kingdom. Second assumption: that they didn't now have it. Third assumption: that one day they would get it back again. Fourth assumption: that Jesus was the King and the one to do it. These four premises lay behind the question, *and Jesus didn't question any of them.*

So I want to warn you: the idea that now the church has

got the kingdom and Israel has lost it will lead you to pride and arrogance, which is totally out of place. As Paul says in Romans 11, the church could lose it and Israel could have it back again.

The kingdom is given to those who produce the fruits of it. The assumption that the organised denominations make – that they have the Holy Spirit, that they have the kingdom, that everything belongs to the church – is a most dangerous assumption, and there are empty church buildings all over the British Isles to prove it, where God has written "Ichabod"[1] over them and said they are not his kingdom.

We should realise that you will only stand by faith in the kingdom, but it was almost as if Jesus was saying: change of plan – instead of establishing the kingdom in Israel and having all the Gentiles come to it, I am going to send you Jews to the ends of the earth to bring the Gentiles in. We now know that it is God's plan to bring the full number of Gentiles in and then to go back and pick up the nation of Israel and bring them in too. God, in his sovereignty, has decided to reverse the order.

In the Old Testament it looked as if God was going to establish the mountain of the Lord in Jerusalem, and that he would be king there and the Gentiles would come. But he let them know this: you will be baptised with the Holy Spirit; you will be my witnesses to the ends of the earth, beginning here in Jerusalem, but I am going to have the international kingdom established first and then we will come back here and bring them in. What an amazing plan! So he sent the disciples out, but he let them know that if they were to be his subjects and to demonstrate his sovereignty, they would do neither without the Holy Spirit. They were to wait in Jerusalem until the Holy Spirit came on them and then they were to go out. That is where the kingdom lies now – wherever the Holy Spirit is.

Wherever the Holy Spirit is filling people, you will see two things: the sovereignty of God being exercised – the same sovereignty Jesus exercised over demons and disease – and you will see people whom the Holy Spirit has enabled to be subjects of the kingdom. The Holy Spirit doesn't just bring the *sovereignty* of the kingdom, he also helps us to be *subjects*. That is the kingdom of Jesus.

Note

[1] *Ichabod* – Meaning "Where is the glory?", implying that the glory had departed. See 1 Samuel 4:21ff.

5

THE KINGDOM AND THE HOLY SPIRIT

Read Acts 1:1–9; *14:21–22*; *28:23 – end*; *Romans 14:17–18*;
Galatians 5:16–17; Colossians 1:9–14.

We have seen that the Christian has a choice every day of
living in the Spirit or living in the flesh, and is free to make
that choice. Do you know what the greatest freedom is? Most
of us, in our youth, thought the greatest freedom was to do
what we wanted, but the greatest freedom is not to do what
you want. To put it another way, *true freedom is freedom
not to sin*, and only those who live in the Spirit know that
freedom – nobody else does.

Paul wrote: "But if you are led by the Spirit, you are not
under law." In other words, if the Spirit is telling you what
to do and you do it, nobody will ever need to tell you about
laws. You won't need to be given rules for your life. You
can be quite sure you won't break any rules if the fruit of
the Spirit is growing. By the way, the fruit of the Spirit is
singular, whereas works of the flesh are plural – there are
many. Any of the works of the flesh could appear in you just
by themselves, but the fruit of the Spirit is one fruit with
nine flavours and you cannot have one of these nine things
without the other eight. They grow together. The fruit of
the Spirit is love, joy, peace, patience, kindness, goodness,
faithfulness, meekness, self-control, and all those things
appear in the life of someone who is living by the Spirit. So
you don't need to *try*, saying, "Well, I'll try and love this
year, and next year I'll try and get a bit of joy, and next year

I'll try to get a bit of peace and the next year I'll really make a New Year's resolution to be more patient. The flesh can reproduce some of those flavours as a kind of substitute – some people are really happy and joyful, but you will find a number of the other flavours missing. Some people are very placid in temperament and very peaceful, so they show peace, but you may find they don't show much self-control.

So you will only find all these nine things appearing together in a life that is living in the Spirit — and that is the secret of a *character*. Those who live in the Spirit will produce all those things. They will grow. Not immediately – they grow gradually and they ripen. It takes time. The *gifts* of the Spirit can appear immediately. The fruit will grow as on a fruit tree over a period, as you live in the Spirit: "those who belong to Christ Jesus have crucified the sinful nature with its passions and desires. Since we live by the Spirit, let us keep in step with the Spirit."

Even during our Lord's ministry on earth, he had already linked together the kingdom and the Spirit. An oft-quoted text is: "Except a man is born again, he cannot see the kingdom of God." What is it to be "born again"? I have heard many, many sermons on "born again", and not one of them ever mentioned water, yet Jesus says to be born again is to be born of water and Spirit, and Nicodemus would have no doubt whatever what he was referring to. He would immediately think of baptism, because the Pharisees to whom Nicodemus belonged were refusing to be baptised. There is an outside and an inside to being born again, and baptism is important. Except a man be born from above – born again, not entering into his mother's womb and going through all that again, but being born of water and Spirit – that is how Jesus defined being born again. It is important that he used two words there – "water and Spirit" – they are both part of being born again. So Jesus already linked them there. He also linked the kingdom and the Spirit when he cast out demons. He said, "If I, by the Spirit of God, cast out demons, then the kingdom of God has come upon you." You will find many such links in the life of Jesus between the kingdom and the Spirit. In fact, he was only able to bring the kingdom as he did because he had been anointed with the Holy Spirit at his baptism. Before he had been anointed himself with the Holy Spirit, he did not release a single person from disease or from demons. He did not perform a single miracle. He just made chairs and tables and door frames with his hands. It was when he was anointed with power in the Holy Spirit that he began to go about doing good. So even Jesus himself could not have re-established the kingdom of God on earth in power without the Holy Spirit. Therefore, when he left earth and the heavens received him again, the disciples might have thought, "Well, that's goodbye to the King and goodbye to the kingdom," but he had other plans. His plans were that just as he had been anointed with power at the age of thirty and then began to demonstrate the kingdom, they would also have an anointing with power in the Holy Spirit and repeat what he had done: they would heal the sick, they would raise the dead, they would release people from demons, and they would demonstrate the kingdom with power.

It has been said: if a man could be filled with the same Holy Spirit that enabled Jesus to do what he did, what could that man not do? It is breathtaking. Jesus said, "The works that I do, you'll do – and even greater." I still cannot come to terms with that statement. I keep wondering what "greater" means. In *scale* I can understand a bit of that. Isn't it amazing that Jesus should have said what he said? The power he was going to give disciples who will carry on the business – doing it through them! What he began to do and teach was not stopping, but now he would do it through them – they were to wait in Jerusalem until they had the power that he had.

So there is a very real sense in which, in our era, the kingdom is wherever the Spirit is. There was a time when I hardly ever heard church people talk about the Holy Spirit in normal conversation, and some of them never even talked about Jesus. You always talk about those whom you know. But there came a time in the twentieth century when the Holy Spirit became a topic of normal conversation – because people got to know him. A few years later, many started using the word "kingdom". Why? Because to discover the Spirit is to discover the kingdom. Now remember that the kingdom is made up of *sovereign* and *subject*. You find that when the Holy Spirit really is given freedom to move, you see two things demonstrated. You see the sovereignty of the kingdom demonstrated, and you will see also subjects of the kingdom, because the Holy Spirit is the one who brings both to us now. You remember the double offer: not only does God offer us *release* by his sovereignty, he is also offering us his *righteousness* to be a subject. In the Spirit, if you walk in the Spirit and live in the Spirit, you will find you don't do the things that the flesh wanted to do, because the two are incompatible.

"Those who are in Christ Jesus have crucified the flesh with its desires." Do you realise that the word "crucified" does not mean "killed"? It means to nail to a cross, but it takes a long time for someone who is crucified to die. Jesus was crucified at nine o'clock in the morning, but he did not die until three o'clock in the afternoon. That was very quick. Most people crucified took three or four days. Some took seven days. The verse that says you have crucified the flesh means you have nailed the flesh to the cross, but the problem is that it takes some time for the flesh to die. The flesh says, "Take the nails out for this afternoon; please just give me a break." If you take the nails out, it can be very much alive again. *You leave your old life on the cross until it is dead.* It has been crucified; it has been nailed there, so leave it there and walk in the Spirit. If you want to enjoy being a subject of the kingdom so that you want to do the right thing – so that you want to keep the commandments; so that you *want* to do it – then the simple thing is to *walk* in the Spirit. There is a place for jumping in the Spirit, there is a place for dancing in the Spirit, but you do not enjoy being a subject of the kingdom just by jumping in the Spirit or dancing in the Spirit – you *walk* in the Spirit to enjoy this. Walking is a fairly simple thing. You just lift one foot and put it down, and then you lift the other and put it down. Walking is not very spectacular. When I go on a country walk I don't jump or dance down the country lane, I just walk. Every step is in a direction I have chosen. Now you can choose to walk in the flesh today or you can choose to walk in the Spirit.

When you have a step to take or a decision to make, if you say "Right, Holy Spirit, which is your way?" and you choose to take another step in that direction, you will enjoy the power of the kingdom. You will express it from time to time in jumping, dancing, or singing in the Spirit or in other ways, but the Bible is quite clear. It is walking in the Spirit that produces the fruit of the Spirit: it is taking one step after another in the direction that he is leading you, that is all.

The Lord is looking for subjects of the kingdom. He is looking for people like you who will determine that you will follow the Spirit wherever he leads. People ask, "Should I leave a place, or should I stay?" The answer is: Do what the Spirit leads you to do. "Whatever the Spirit clearly leads me to do, I will do" – that is all you need to decide, to be a subject of the kingdom, but I have the feeling that many people's experience of the Holy Spirit has faded because at some point he was leading them to take a step which they were unwilling to take.

I know that I don't go wrong through ignorance, I

go wrong through disobedience. I don't talk about the charismatic renewal fading or dying. I can see that in some people and in some churches it is fading and dying because there came a point where they said, "No further, I'm not prepared to take that step" – and of course their experience faded. But, praise God, I meet hundreds of people who are stepping out and saying, "I'll still take every step the Spirit leads me to take." But you need to be sure that it is the Spirit. There are impulses of the flesh we need to watch and there are suggestions from other people, so we are told to check everything out carefully. All that God is asking from you is that you promise him that everything you know the Spirit leads you to do, you will do, and you are a subject of his kingdom. The kingdom of God will be yours. Righteousness and peace and joy will be yours and you are free.

The two dangers for all Christians are legalism and licence. Have you ever been on one of those paths like Striding Edge in the Lake District up on Helvellyn where two big ice balls in the Ice Age have ground themselves into what we call "corries", great hollows, and have left a sharp edge of rock? You can walk along the top, but when the wind gets up you almost have to be on your knees. I see the Christian life as walking along such an edge. On the one hand is the danger of dropping into legalism – and isn't it awful to go into a fellowship that has become legalistic, where they are constantly setting rules for each other: don't do this, don't do that. There is a kind of dreadful atmosphere. I have been into churches and assemblies and fellowships that have turned legalistic and somehow it has all become a matter of regulation, imposed standards and law. The people must dress in a certain way. There is an oppressive spirit because there is legalism.

On the other hand, I have also met people who slip down the other slope into licence, and who think, "Well now, I'm a Christian, I've got my ticket to glory, I can do what I like – I can go on sinning." Paul says to those who have fallen into licence, to Christians who think they can do what they like, "I've warned you before. Those who go on doing those things will not inherit the kingdom."

So what's the answer? The answer is neither legalism nor licence. There is the liberty of the Spirit which is a very delicately balanced path in between both those things, where you are free in the Spirit to walk in the Spirit, to follow the Spirit – and it is real freedom. You are free from legalism and you are free from licence because both of those things are sheer slavery. In legalism, you become a slave to other people. In licence, you become a slave to yourself. In the Spirit, you are free. This is the kingdom of God, in which we may now live. I am amazed. The good news is: you can live in the kingdom of heaven today. I can live in the kingdom of heaven! I can be sovereign and subject in the Spirit, with power to live right.

I cannot help noticing that through Acts and the epistles the emphasis is still on finding *subjects* for the kingdom. It is almost as if Jesus said: now you have got the Spirit; you must go everywhere in the world and do what I have been doing in Israel; you must set people free from Satan, but what you are really after is to bring them into the kingdom as my subjects. Go into all the world. Make disciples of all nations, baptising them and teaching them how to do everything I have taught you.

The ultimate target of evangelism is to produce a man or a woman who is able to do everything Jesus commanded. What a remarkable task! We have whittled evangelism down to making decisions, but I believe that what Jesus sent us to do was not to get people to make decisions, but to make disciples, which means to bring them right through to the point where they can do and want to do everything Jesus told us. You will never do that without introducing them to the Holy Spirit.

I believe we won't get back to the evangelism that Jesus wanted until the evangelist talks about being baptised in water and baptised in the Holy Spirit, and when these are a vital part of counselling every new believer. It is ten times easier for a new convert to be filled with the Spirit than a Christian who has been going for twenty-five years without that – they are wide open.

I believe what God wants is that every person who comes forward to make a decision be introduced to the Holy Spirit; that instead of saying "Receive Jesus", which the New Testament never says, instead of saying, "Receive Jesus as your Saviour" or, "Receive him into your heart" or "Receive him into your life", we stop talking like that which is unscriptural, and we go back to the kind of evangelistic preaching in the Bible that says, "Repent toward God, believe in the Lord Jesus, and receive the Holy Spirit."

Not one evangelistic sermon in the New Testament ever told people to receive Jesus – so stop using that term. You can't receive Jesus; he is not around to receive. The heavens have received him now. Of course, when he was on earth in the flesh you could receive him. You could open your door and say, "Come in, Jesus." When he came in the flesh, he came to his own people, the Jews, and I am afraid they did not receive him. Those who did were given the power to become sons of God, but that verse in John's Gospel is not an evangelistic verse, it is a description of what happened when Jesus was on earth.

From the day that he was received back into the heavens, they never told people to receive Jesus ever again. His place on earth has been taken by the Holy Spirit. He is the one you receive now. *Believe* on the Lord Jesus and *receive* the Holy Spirit. Therefore, that was why Paul was desperately concerned about people whom he thought had believed without receiving. "Did you receive the Holy Spirit when you believed?" He wanted to make sure that people had a firsthand introduction.

I confess that my initiation into the kingdom was spread over far too long a time. It was years before someone talked to me about baptism in water. I am glad I caught up on it, but I wished somebody had told me about that when I was converted. It would have been so much more appropriate. Some people say, "Oh well, it's too late now. I've been a Christian twenty years. What's the point?" Well, it is always right to put things right.

I have led men and women to the Lord who have been living together for years and were not married. They could have said, "What's the point of getting married now?" but I always marry people like that and get the thing regularised. Yes, their wedding hasn't quite the same feel as it might have had if it had taken place at the beginning, but it is vital that they put the thing right and be properly married in the sight of the Lord and in the sight of other people. If you say, "Well I've been a believer thirty years; it's a bit late to get baptised now," it is right to put it right, even if it doesn't feel the same as if it had been there at the beginning.

Likewise, it was years before I heard about being baptised in the Spirit. Praise God, he is so patient that his Spirit had blessed me and used me and regenerated me and done everything, and then I found out years after I became a Christian that you could be filled to overflowing. I wish somebody had told me at the beginning. I would have had a better start. I believe that God is wanting us to bring people right into the fullness of the kingdom at the very start of their Christian life. Most of us have to catch up on these things over a period of years. Let us put it together again. Let us put repentance, faith, baptism and being filled with the Spirit into the package deal for every believer, and we are going to see Christians who will race past us!

Visiting New Zealand once, I learnt that Dunedin was home to many Presbyterians. "Dunedin" means "New Edin" and it is "new Edinburgh" where the Scottish migrants settled. When Presbyterianism loses its life it becomes very heavy. Calvinism is a deadening thing if you lose the faith that Calvin had. They said to me, "Nothing happens here. We never have big meetings because it's the evangelists' graveyard." So they had booked for me the main theatre in the middle of Dunedin for two nights. On the first night the city lived up to its reputation. It was heavy going, with nothing much happening, except that I met one remarkable man in his early thirties. His name was Wayne and he had only been a Christian for three weeks. He was converted and filled with the Holy Spirit in one fell swoop, in one day, without any church background, without any Christian help. I sat at his feet and I learned from him. He had been filled with the Spirit, and that same night he went to bed and was so excited. He slept soundly until three in the morning and then he woke up. He said, "David, there was an angel standing at the foot of my bed," so I tried to look as if that happened most nights to me, and I sort of said, "What happened then?"

"Well," he said, "He spoke to me. I think I was rather rude to him because I'm not used to talking to angels."

"Well, what did he say?"

He said, "Wayne, today is your special day."

Wayne said, "You got your clock wrong, mate. It's three in the morning. Yesterday was my special day."

The angel said, "Wayne, you're not listening. Today is your special day."

He said, "Why? What's going to happen today? Is my wife going to get converted today?" She was lying in bed alongside him, asleep.

The angel said, "Wayne, listen. Today is your special day."

Wayne turned to me at this point and said, "David, I realised what he was trying to say—that I mustn't live on yesterday's experience."

Now fancy learning that at three in the morning the day after your conversion! Most Christians haven't learned that yet. Ask them to give their testimony and they talk about twenty years ago.

Wayne said, "Every day I wake up and I say: Wayne, today is your special day!"

For three weeks, he'd had twenty-one special days.

I must tell you one other thing about him. I said, "Wayne, we're not getting anywhere in this town are we? We've got to have a prayer meeting before tonight's or tomorrow night's thing," so there was Wayne and about thirty others and we prayed, "Lord, give us a breakthrough tonight. In Dunedin of all places, give us a breakthrough", and we got it. I don't know how many people were counselled that night – maybe a couple of hundred – but it was such a response in that dead place. After the meeting was over and everybody had gone home, there were only two people left in the building: the Presbyterian minister who had organised it, and Wayne.

Wayne went into the theatre foyer to go out and go home and he felt the Lord forbade him to go through those glass doors into the street. He stopped and said, "Can't I go home?"

"No."

"But Lord, what? Are you trying to say something? What are you trying to say? I can't hear what you're trying to say." He couldn't get through. So finally he said, "Lord, please could I just go out for a breath of fresh air? I'll walk round the block. I'll promise to come back in and then I'll listen to you."

He said, "The Lord gave me permission." So he walked round the square, came back in, stood in the foyer and asked,

"Now Lord, what was it?" and the Lord told him.

Wayne got hold of the Presbyterian minister and took him back into the prayer room where we had been before the service. He spoke to that minister, "Kneel down. Get on your knees," and he knelt with him. He continued, "I hope you don't think this is critical, but the Lord wouldn't let me go out of the foyer tonight and he said he's got something to say, and what he said to me was this — "Wayne, they asked me for a breakthrough. I gave it to them, but no-one came back to say 'thank you.'"

So Wayne said, "Come on, let's say thank you." This is a three-week old spiritual baby. I tell you, I spent every minute I could with him, drinking in from him what the Lord was teaching him. Let us not rob new Christians of the power of the kingdom through the Holy Spirit. Why do we have to wait till we have read a book or gone to a conference before we enjoy that power? I want to encourage you: everybody who comes to Christ within reach of you, introduce them to the power of the kingdom through the Holy Spirit. Teach them how to walk in the Spirit. Don't give them a list of rules. Teach them how to respond to the Spirit.

I remember one particular lady who started attending our church. She came to Christ. She came to me afterwards and said, "I've got a problem."

I said, "What's your problem?"

"My job."

I asked, "What's your job?"

She told me, "I'm the proprietor of a chain of betting shops."

"Well, what's your problem?"

"Well, I'm a Christian now. What do I do about it?" She said, "It's a really good business because it is in Aldershot, the home of the British Army."

Can you imagine? It was a little gold mine to run a chain

of betting shops there. She said, "Should I be doing this as a Christian?"

I replied, "I'm not going to tell you."

"Oh," she said, "You're the sixth person in the church I've asked and they've all said the same thing." She was quite frustrated. I was thrilled that nobody in our church told her she must not do that and didn't bring her under legalism by making rules for her.

"How do I find out?" she asked me.

I replied, "Well, try sharing the business with Jesus for a week."

"How do I do that?"

"You keep talking to him as you take the money off the soldiers. You just say, 'Jesus how do you feel about this, taking this money?' And as you make up the books at the end of the day and find out how much profit you have made, say, 'Jesus, how do you like that?' Try it for a week. Just share the business with him."

She came back the next Sunday and said, "It's been a disaster. All the books have gone wrong. We haven't even made a profit this week. It's been one disaster area after another." She sold the business and bought a tea shop!

We must trust the Spirit more to lead, instead of making rules for people and getting them into legalism, or falling the other way and saying, "Oh, you've got your ticket to heaven, you're forgiven – do what you like." Let's be honest and tell them about the Spirit—how to walk in the Spirit; how to be led in the Spirit; how to enjoy the kingdom.

So far, I have been concentrating almost exclusively on the individual walking in the Spirit, but in Galatians 6 the word "walk" [in the Spirit] occurs twice. The first time the word "walk" means to walk by *yourself* in the Spirit; but the second time is about *marching in step*. The New Testament shows clearly that the kingdom is to be enjoyed *together*.

Walking in the Spirit is not something you will manage on your own – it is keeping in step with others who are walking in the Spirit. One of the reasons some believers may not be enjoying as much of the Spirit and his power as they might, is that they are trying to do it on their own. Some are having to, if they are too far from other Spirit-filled Christians. If that is you, then pray that the Lord will show you what to do about it. It might be that you have not found those you need to find in the area where you live.

It is quite clear that it was Jesus' intention not just to have a lot of subjects walking in the Spirit by themselves, but that they be communities in the Spirit; that they enjoy fellowship in the Spirit. I do not think I would have been here today if I had not had fellowship in the Spirit with others also walking in the Spirit. Is that not true? God never intended you to do it on your own, and that is why when he was looking for subjects of the kingdom, he called twelve to be the nucleus. They had to live and walk as a group, sharing their lives with each other; and when you look at them, they were the most unlikely mix of people you could imagine. Yet on the night before Jesus died, he said: one thing that I want you to do – love each other.

The power of the Spirit is the power not only to cause an individual to live right and be a subject, but the power of the Spirit is the power to get on with the most unlikely people and be a harmonious community in the Spirit – in other words, the church – not the building down the road with a steeple and bells, but the people inhabited by the Spirit of God. The church is people.

Some Christians are guilty of misguided loyalty. What I am going to point out may be misunderstood and misquoted, but I need to affirm it: God never called you to be loyal to a denomination, because he doesn't even think "denomination". He called you to be loyal to him and to his body, not to a denomination. Nor did he ever call you to be loyal to a minister. Nor did he ever call you to be loyal to a church building. But there are Christians who are held up all over the place because of misguided loyalty. They have put that loyalty before their loyalty to the King and their loyalty to his other subjects. To move from one denomination to another may simply mean to move from one part of his body to another. I believe many Christians need to be finding their place in the body where they will be fulfilled, matured and developed – because so many of their gifts are being held back since they are never used. The things they are discovering in the Spirit are being lost because they are never expressed. Do you think that is the will of God? There is a misguided loyalty. Now if the Lord has told you to stay in that denomination and in that church building and with that minister, that is different – but you are doing it out of loyalty to the King, not out of loyalty to them. If the Lord tells you to shift to another part of his body where he can fit you in and develop you and grow you and use your gifts, that is not disloyalty to the part you are leaving. You are still loyal to the King and to his kingdom, but you need to find the community in which he meant you to be. You need to find other Spirit-filled people and, above all, you need to be under Spirit-filled leadership—that is an absolute must. You cannot have a community without leadership, and you cannot have a Spirit-led community that is not led by Spirit-led leaders.

When I was in Australia, I went to a place for one night at the invitation of a young farmer who had faith to book the town hall – which had never been booked for a religious meeting in that little one-horse town which was largely engaged in agricultural marketing. There were a few little churches, but they had never seen a large gathering of Christians. This young farmer got in touch with me and he said, "Will you come? I've booked the town hall which seats eleven hundred." So I went. We had a revival! It was packed, people had come fifty and sixty miles, including many farmers. There were eleven hundred people there. Before the evening, the Holy Spirit spoke to us and said, "I have given you this town." You wonder what can happen in one night, but I tell you the sound of weeping in that hall could be heard down the High Street. The Spirit came down on the meeting. I looked at all these people – so eager, so hungry, it was the first time they had seen anything like it. I thought: but I've got to leave tomorrow morning. What can I do to help them to keep what they have found? I said, "Lord, have you got a word for them?" and he gave me a prophetic word. When I get a prophetic word, it is usually no longer than one sentence, but it is usually so clear and so simple that people get it. Others may have longer words from the Lord, but I tend to get sometimes a phrase that just puts it right on the spot. I heard a sentence from God. I said, "Listen, God has begun to move in this place and you may be wondering: where do you go from here? How do you follow through? How do you keep what he's giving you? Here's his word for you: 'Follow the men who follow the Lord.'" That was all.

I said, "I'm going to look around and I'm going to ask the Lord to show me the men who are led by the Spirit in this place," and he showed me three men. I knew they were the men who were being led by the Spirit and I said, "Follow these men." Now you can imagine what a furore that caused because there were more churches than three. But God's way of establishing his kingdom has always been through men led by the Spirit and people willing to follow men led by the Spirit. Some believers need to hear that. How will the kingdom be established if you follow men who are not led by the Spirit, who are therefore not experiencing the kingdom themselves? Do not let misguided loyalty prevent you from following the men who follow the Lord. It is why I like to spend time with leaders. Just because a man turns his collar back to front and has degrees after his name does not mean that is the one you have got to follow. I am expressing this bluntly and plainly, because I want to see the kingdom established wherever you are. You can empty the church by degrees, did you know that? I have got some myself, so I am not just being envious or knocking other people.

You need to be aware that the qualification for leadership in the kingdom is that a man is led by the Spirit. It is the only qualification I know. What I see happening all over England is that God is raising up people from many different walks of life, filling them with his Spirit and making them leaders of his kingdom. You will need to recognise those leaders and follow them even though they may never have been near a theological "cemetery" (I use those words deliberately).

If we are to march together as an army, if we are to be a community in the kingdom, then we are going to need Spirit-led leaders to follow. If you are not led by a Spirit-led leader, then I would ask you to ask the Lord to show you how you can get in line with God's purposes. That is the way it happened all through the Bible. There comes a man from God, and the people follow. When no man had enough courage, and Deborah stepped in and had to take decisions for the people of God, she told them: because no man would take the lead, then God will give Sisera into the hands of a woman – and he did. You can read the account in the book of Judges, but after the whole thing was over, after Sisera was defeated, Deborah sang a song to the Lord and this was her song: "That the leaders led and that the people followed, praise the Lord." That was her praise; that is how the kingdom happens. When God raises up a leader full of his Spirit and led by his Spirit, he expects his people to follow. Not in a slavish way, though. We are not called to authoritarianism.

So the key, I believe, to the establishment of the kingdom is going to be Spirit-led leaders, and if you have not got them around, you should be praying very hard: "Lord, will you fill men with your Holy Spirit so that they are led by you and we can get behind them." That is how it will happen.

What I have just been explaining here, even if it is properly understood and properly quoted, will have an offensiveness in it. I am prepared to be shot at. I am prepared to take that offence, but I must be honest before the Lord. The kingdom comes through Spirit-led believers getting behind Spirit-led leaders and there is no other way, because God cannot bring the kingdom just with one individual here and another there and another there who have been baptised in the Spirit and who enjoy edifying themselves in tongues and then sit in a dead situation, sitting on all the other gifts they might have used or been given. That will not operate. For some Christians it will mean that you have to ask the Lord where you have to live. Maybe he wants you to move house to where you can get in line with what he is doing, but that is for him to say. I find a great freedom when I am counselling people and saying, "It's not for me to tell you. It's for you to be willing to be a subject of the King. I'll help you to be, but in the last analysis you must seek his will."

That is a serious note on which to finish this Chapter, and I realise that may put some people on the spot. I do not apologise for that, because I would be more hurt if I left you in a situation where you are going to suppress your gifts; where you are not going to develop what the Spirit is doing in you; where you are going to be, as it were, useless to the kingdom because you are not in a community of the Spirit, where together you can keep in step and march in the Spirit.

6

THE PROSPECTS FOR THE KINGDOM

Please read Revelation 1:4–8; 5:6–10; 11:15–17; 19:11–16; 20:4–6; 22:1–6.

The kingdom is a huge subject and, as we have seen, the theme that links together the whole Bible is the re-establishment of the kingdom of God on earth.

In Revelation chapter 1 we find the description of Jesus as "the ruler of the kings of the earth". That means he rules over Presidents, Prime Ministers and other world leaders. So when you read your newspapers, just say, "I know the person who rules them. He's in charge."

How will it all end? Some years ago, at a kind of house party, a businessman started chatting with me. He said, "What's your job?" I said, "I'm the minister of a church." He looked at me with pity in his eyes and said, "What's it feel like to belong to a dying organisation?"

"I wouldn't know."

"Come off it," he said, "the church is dying everywhere. I see church buildings closed down and made into other things."

I responded, "The church I belong to isn't dying."

"Which church is that?"

"The church of Jesus Christ." He looked a little taken aback, but I pressed home the advantage and said, "Now listen, did you know that the church of Jesus Christ has a net gain, even allowing for deaths, of something like a thousand people an hour or in round terms, twenty-five thousand extra every day. If your business was getting twenty-five thousand new customers a day, would you talk about a dying organisation?"

Quite impressed with that, he replied, "No, I guess not."

But I lost him when I said, "The church is the only society on earth that never loses a single member by death." He looked at me as much as to say, "Oh, he's one of those cranks," and walked away!

That encounter was many decades ago and those figures are way out of date. The net increase to the church of Jesus Christ every single day is now vastly greater, even allowing for deaths. We do not belong to a dying organisation. The church of Christ has never grown as quickly as it is growing today – not in two thousand years has there been such an amazing increase. It is happening because Jesus said, "I will build my church." I am so glad he did not tell me to build it but said, "I will build it" – and he is doing a very good job. The number of Christians in Africa and Asia increased particularly dramatically in the past few decades. In Korea, India, China, South America and many other places the number of committed Christian believers is growing. We are in a kingdom that is getting established. But have you noticed that the headquarters of the kingdom of God on earth has moved to the developing world? Our pride in these islands is that we love to support missionaries over *there*, but we now need and welcome missionaries from many other countries.

You may never have realised that the kingdom is growing so fast. Historically, most missionaries went out from Europe and America, so why is the kingdom not growing in the Western world today? The main reason why it is hard to talk about the kingdom here, I can sum up in one sentence: Jesus said, "It is hard for a rich man to enter the kingdom of heaven." By New Testament standards, most us in the

UK are rich. The amount of money we get through in a year would have kept somebody in the New Testament going for a lifetime. Jesus dared to tell them, with a tiny sum to live on, "Seek first the kingdom of God and his righteousness and you'll always have enough to eat and enough to wear." Can you imagine preaching that to people who are trying to live on a pound or so a day?

We used to live just half a mile from an Elizabethan mansion in Surrey, where a well-known millionaire lived. When we heard the word "rich" we always thought of him. There he was with his fantastic millions, yet he had a coin slot machine for his telephone in the guest bedroom because all his guests used to ring up their friends in New Zealand whenever they stayed. It was said that his secretary had orders to give five pounds to everybody who asked him for charity, so you could always get five pounds out of him, but he was worth millions.

Now when you read the word "rich" in the Bible, you are not to think of millionaires, you are to think of yourself. Frankly, the British are much too rich – it is hard for them to enter the kingdom of God. There are far too many other things they can buy, far too many other things they can enjoy, far too many electronic devices, far too many holidays abroad. So the kingdom of God has moved to the developing world. I find that interesting.

The wealthy West will have to say, "Send missionaries to us, please. Send men to teach us about the kingdom." We would love to have a revival all our own that is nice and British. I don't think it is going to happen that way. We are going to have to humble ourselves and go to those who know much more about the kingdom than we do. But from God's point of view, the kingdom is growing. The mustard seed has become a mighty tree already, and the birds of the air are nesting in it. That phrase in Scripture always means the Gentiles, the nations. You find it in the Old Testament and the New: the picture of a tree with the birds of the air coming and lodging in it is the picture of the nations coming into the kingdom of God.

Jesus said that the kingdom is like a little bit of yeast, which a woman hid in a lump of dough, but it spread through the whole lump and it affected the whole lot. Jesus expected the kingdom to grow. I just want to reassure you that it is growing faster today than it has ever grown before. New subjects of the kingdom are pouring in – praise the Lord for that. Rejoice at what is happening on a world scale and count it a privilege to be a tiny part of that big thing. I would not like to estimate how many hundreds of millions because, as I told you, we never lose anybody by death; they are just transferred to another branch.

What, then, is the likely outcome of all this? Are we going to see the church grow to such an extent that in fact it will take over the world? Are we likely to see the number of Christians multiply so rapidly now that there will be nobody else left, that we will just swamp everything else and be able to take over the government of every nation? Well, no. Will we ever see God's government visibly established on earth? Jesus taught us to pray every single day, "Your kingdom come ... on earth as it is in heaven." But there are very few Christians in our nation, I believe, actually looking forward to that happening. As I pointed out earlier, most Christians seem to think our job is to rescue a few individuals and deliver them safely to heaven. Our hope for the future does not seem to include earth. We seem to have got so concentrated on heaven, and getting a few more people to heaven, that we have lost all hope of the kingdom being established here on earth – despite Jesus having told us to pray for that.

I suggest that when you read your New Testament you

start underlining the word "earth". You will be astonished how earthly the New Testament is. Yes, we need to think of heaven, but I am just pointing to the fact that God's kingdom is to come on earth. "Blessed are the poor in spirit," said Jesus, "For they will inherit the kingdom of heaven." In the very next breath he said, "And blessed are the meek, for they shall inherit the earth." God is not going to give up part of his universe. He would not be content to have heaven fall and write earth off – because he made heaven and earth and he is going to redeem heaven and earth. He is going to re-establish his kingdom through the whole lot.

The range of Christian opinion about what we expect to happen on earth through the growth of the church varies from extreme pessimism to extreme optimism. There is an extremely pessimistic view of the future which I have found among many believers. The pessimistic view goes something like this: "We're in the last days and things are getting worse and worse. There is going to be a great falling away. There will only be you and me left and I am not so sure if you are sound. We must just wait for the king to come back because things are going to get worse and worse until he comes." Have you heard that kind of pessimism? I am caricaturing it, but you would be amazed how many who claim to believe the New Testament talk in pessimistic terms like that and have resigned themselves to having a little assembly that will get smaller and smaller. That is not the New Testament. The New Testament is not pessimistic about the church, but at the other end of the scale, there is in many liberal churches – and there was in many of the missionary hymns of the nineteenth century – a naïve optimism at the other end of the scale, which talked as if, with a great imperial missionary effort, the church was going to take the world over. I love the story of the drunk and the Salvation Army officer on the train from Edinburgh down to London. The drunk said to the Salvation Army officer, "What have you been doing?" The officer said, "I've been fighting the devil in Aberdeen. I've been fighting the devil in Edinburgh. Now I'm on my way to fight him in Newcastle and I'm going to fight him in York and I'll finish up by fighting him in London." The drunk apparently said to him, "That's right, drive the blighter south!" There is a kind of naïve optimism, which you sometimes find in prayer groups, that believes we are going to drive Satan out of Britain ourselves – that we are really going to take over, and the church is going to push evil out and clean the place up; we are going to root out all traces of the kingdom of Satan. That naïve optimism is not New Testament teaching. So I want to protect you from either the pessimism that will paralyse you or the optimism that will disillusion you. I want to get you into biblical realism that says: "Both kingdoms are going to grow until the King comes back and cleans it up. The wheat is going to grow and the tares are going to grow, and both will become more and more manifest until the end of the age when the king sends his angels in to clear it up." That is realism. The kingdom of God is going to grow, but so is the kingdom of Satan. Any thought that either will conquer the other before the king gets back, I think is not scriptural, not realistic. So I am a realist, neither naively pessimistic, nor naively optimistic.

Let me spell out the realism of the Bible teaching about the prospects for the future of the kingdom. I want to draw a distinction between strategy and tactics. Strategy is the overall objective and ultimate outcome; tactics are how you set about achieving that. Every military commander must have a strategy that he is aiming at, but he must work out his tactics to reach the goal. God's strategy is absolutely clear: it is to bring the whole earth back under his rule. I have no doubt whatever that this earth will one day be totally back under his rule. I am absolutely sure that both Old and New

Testaments are right when they say, "He will be king of the whole earth." Zechariah chapter 14 tells us that – it describes the Messiah's return, when his feet will stand on the Mount of Olives and all the nations will go up to Jerusalem for the Feast of Tabernacles – the one Jewish feast that has not been fulfilled yet. Passover has been fulfilled, Pentecost has been fulfilled, but the Tabernacles hasn't, and it is the feast of the return of the king. Actually, it is the time when Jesus was born also. He was not born on December 25th, I'm sure you knew that, but what you may not have known was that he was born in the middle of the Feast of Tabernacles and "... the word became flesh and tabernacled among us." The evidence for it is all there in your Bible.

At every Feast of Tabernacles, on the first day in synagogues, they read Zechariah 14. It is the only time in the whole year when the Jews pray for the Gentiles. They read Zechariah 14 where it says that his feet will stand on the Mount of Olives and he will be king over the whole earth and the nations will come to Jerusalem for the Feast of Tabernacles. Then they pray like this: "Lord, please bring the Gentiles to Jerusalem for the feast so that Messiah may come."

Incidentally, some decades ago – for the first time in two thousand years – thirty of us Gentiles went for the feast. The Lord told us to come back the next year with six hundred. We went back with 624 Gentiles the second year. The third year, four thousand came. The impact on Israel that the Gentiles had come to Jerusalem for the feast of the coming of the King has been enormous.

The book of Revelation says that the kingdom of the world has become the kingdom of our Lord and of his Christ, and he will reign for ever and ever. That is certain to happen – it is the strategy of God. Because God is sovereign and on the throne, nothing can stop that happening, but it is the kingdom of the world that has become his kingdom, so it is not heaven we are talking about now, it is the kingdom of *this* world.

In 1 Corinthians 15, that marvellous passage on the resurrection, almost as an afterthought or something just slipped in as a bonus, there is this statement: "Then the end will come, when Jesus hands over the kingdom to God the Father, after he has destroyed all authority, dominion, and power." In other words, the strategy of God is that his Son, Jesus, should take over every nation, every state, every authority, every power in this world, and hand it back to his Dad—what a strategy!

The story of the kingdom in the New Testament can be divided into three "chapters". The first "chapter", which you read in the Gospels, centres on the second person of the Trinity. The second "chapter", which you read about in Acts and the epistles, centres on the third person of the Trinity, the Spirit. But the final "chapter" always talks about the kingdom of the Father, and that is where it finishes.

Christ came to make possible the re-establishment of the kingdom on earth; he then returned to heaven and sent the Spirit to carry on the work; he intends to come back to complete it and hand it all back to Father. What a strategy! That is the framework of the entire New Testament. All the teaching it gives us about family life, about how we handle our money, how we handle our sex, how we handle everything else – all that teaching is in the context of that overall strategy. Sometimes I think we get so bogged down in the little bits that we lose sight of what it is all about. To get your family life straight, to get your private life straight, is all part of a huge strategy to re-establish the kingdom on earth.

Now what about the tactics? We know the overall strategy, but how will he do it? In particular, I want to ask questions like these: Will this happen through the church or independently of the church? Will it be a gradual process or a sudden crisis? Will it be by earthly infiltration or by heavenly invasion? Will the Lord use men or angels to do this? Will he use human or heavenly agents? Or, to put it bluntly, will the kingdom be re-established on earth before the King returns or after? Listing such questions, you will realise that I am walking through a minefield. It is called eschatology, meaning simply the study of the last things. You know that as soon as you raise the last things, you are going to upset somebody. So I realise that I am going to tread on corns here. A friend of mine went to Belfast and they asked him at the airport when he got off the plane, "Are you pre-millennial, postmillennial or amillennial?" He said, "That is a-pre-post-erous question and I'm not going to answer it!" I am sad that Christians can divide from one another over the future. I have a lot of sympathy with people who say, "I'm pan-millennial, which means it'll all pan out alright in the end." But, seriously, I believe that God has revealed things to us that we need to study and look at.

I am going to give my own understanding of the scripture and I simply ask you neither to accept what I say nor reject it, but to check it out. Do what the Bereans did when Paul argued from the scriptures: they searched the scriptures to see whether these things were so. Try to free your mind from the timetable you were brought up with. You can unconsciously assume that only one view of the future is sound.

So what are the tactics? Will the kingdom be re-established by the church before Jesus comes back or by the angels when he does come back? Will it be a gradual infiltration of the whole world by Christians or will it be a sudden invasion from heaven, an apocalyptic crisis? Christians have asked these questions for much of the past two thousand years and I will give you my answer very simply in one word: *both*. Will the kingdom be established by a sudden crisis or a gradual process? Both. Will the kingdom be established before or after Jesus gets back? Both. Will the kingdom be established by human or heavenly agents? Both.

Did you know that out of the many parables that Jesus told about the kingdom (about sixty altogether), half of them describe a present-gradual process of growth. Exactly half of them describe a future sudden crisis. Yet, they are all about the kingdom. If Jesus taught fifty-fifty, I am going to teach fifty-fifty. If Jesus said it is both happening – now and then – then I am going to say both.

It means, quite simply, that the kingdom will not be completely re-established on earth by the church. There is a *now* and a *then* about Jesus' teaching on the kingdom, so sometimes you think he is talking about something that will happen at the end of the age, and at other times he is talking about something that is happening right now, and the answer is both. God is already preparing the kingdom. He is already re-establishing it on earth through the growth of the church. He is re-establishing it, but for the complete coming of the kingdom we wait for the return of the king.

Peter, in one of his earlier sermons, taught: Jesus has been received by the heavens until the time of the restoration of all things. Many new fellowships, indeed many Christians, were talking about "restoration" in the twentieth century. Earlier we began to talk about "renewal" and now the word "revival" is often used. But take the word "restoration." Yes, the Lord is restoring his church. He is restoring the patterns he wanted – of family life, church life and evangelism. But don't make the mistake of calling that, "The Restoration". The Restoration is when the King gets back, and the restoration of all things awaits his return. Meanwhile, you can be restored; your family can be restored; your church can be restored to what God meant it to be when he originally made it, but that is not the Restoration. We wait for that, for his return from heaven.

I want to mention very briefly, the kingdom as a present process, a gradual infiltration – for that is the form it is taking now and it is not a very visible form. Even when Jesus was demonstrating the powers of the kingdom, he says, "You can't say, 'the kingdom is here ... it is there.'" The world, and most of the people in your town or city, are quite unaware that the kingdom is being re-established right in their midst. Jesus said that the kingdom is among you – it is in your midst; it is happening.

My wife and I have had the privilege of visiting hundreds of towns and cities around Britain, and there is not one place we have been to where we have not found the kingdom being re-established. It is happening all over the place; it is a kind of secret underground movement. It is like the leaven in the dough. It is like the little mustard seed. People just don't realise that these small things that are happening are part of something that is going to be very big.

I want to lift your morale because I believe that morale is the key to winning or losing the battle. The kingdom *is* being established. We don't see headlines in the newspapers about the kingdom of God. Almost every headline seems to be from the kingdom of Satan. It may look as if he is winning, but the kingdom of God is spreading and growing.

Jesus said that the kingdom is like scattering seed. Three-quarters of it gets wasted. Three-quarters of your proclaiming the kingdom gets wasted. Do you ever feel like that in your evangelism? Don't worry – Jesus felt like that too. He said, "The kingdom is like a sower who went forth to sow and some of it fell on hard ground and some on stony ground." Out of every four grains, only one grew. So why does the farmer bother when so much is wasted? The answer is that from the one that gets into good ground you get thirty or sixty, or even a hundred back.

I remember hearing of a man in Northern Ireland who

conducted an evangelistic crusade and he made appeal after appeal. It was a week's mission and nobody in the whole week responded except one criminal tramp, who happened to drop in one night and listened, and went out, and in the middle of the field was converted. I am not going to mention his name, but he became one of the best known evangelists in the whole of Northern Ireland and he led thousands to the Lord. That evangelist went home thinking the mission had been a waste of time and that there had been no response, but there had been one. His seed fell into good ground in a tramp's heart – one who was a thief. It had been a thousand-fold return. So don't get depressed when your seed falls.

You know that you have to go and proclaim the good news. But the good news is not only how to escape hell – the good news is the good news of the kingdom. Jesus taught us that the gospel of the kingdom will be preached to all the nations and then the end will come. I think it is time we got back to proclaiming Christ as King. Yes, he is our Saviour; yes, he is Lord; yes, he is the healer. But I think it is time we started preaching him as *King* again and proclaim the good news of the kingdom of heaven: you can live in the kingdom now; you can have the sovereignty of the kingdom now; you can become a subject of the kingdom now; you can know the release of the kingdom now; you can live in the righteousness of the kingdom now. You can have the future today—that is the good news of the kingdom.

I believe that there will be an increasing growth in the number of subjects of the kingdom, until every people, every tribe, every nation has the yeast of the kingdom working in it secretly, infiltrating life at so many points.

God is putting Christians in many key situations – into politics, into the entertainment world and the sports world. We often don't know the kingdom is happening. It is like yeast spreading through the lump. There is a base of the kingdom everywhere if you look for it. Sometimes you have to look pretty hard, but it is there, a little base. Don't despise the day of small things—that is the base. Jesus finished up with eleven men, but he did not get depressed. The eleven were enough as a base. Six weeks later, he had got 120 and twenty-four hours after that, he had three thousand. A few weeks after that, he had five thousand. It has gone on like that ever since. The church is growing at a fantastic rate. It will not establish the kingdom fully, but it will plant a base for that kingdom to be established in every tribe, kindred, tongue and people. That is God's tactics. He didn't expect us to take the world over. Indeed, when he comes back, he doesn't expect to find everybody a Christian. I am not declaring that to excuse you from proclaiming the kingdom but just so you don't have false idealism – so that you don't get all worked up. There are some choruses that came out in the 1980s which to my mind were naively optimistic, taking words that apply to the future and applying them to the present. Don't get any false ideas from singing choruses like that – saying that we are going to take the world over. People can get all steamed up with "imperial" ideas: we are on the march and we are going to take the whole lot. Let us be utterly realistic and say: we are in a kingdom that is growing and we are going to establish a base for that kingdom wherever we can. We are going to build colonies of the kingdom wherever we can. It is not a kingdom we are building, it is a colony of the kingdom. We are getting ready for the day the king comes back and takes over the whole lot.

He will do it the second time not by riding on a donkey, but by coming on a white horse. The difference between a donkey and the white horse is that when you ride on a donkey you come in peace; when you ride on a white horse you come in war. The King of kings will come on a white horse and establish the kingdom worldwide. Why did he not come on a white horse the first time? Because he wanted to give us a chance to be voluntarily subjects – but God has set a day when that opportunity will end, and when the kingdom will be established anyway.

Now we come to the second part of God's tactics. The first part is the present process of growth and infiltration, of establishing colonies of the kingdom of heaven everywhere we can, to be ready for the day – because it is God's strategy that in his kingdom there will be people of every tribe, language and nation. No part of the human race will be missing from his kingdom – so we had better get them ready, hadn't we? In a sense we are like John the Baptist, getting people ready for the King. The other part of God's tactics will be a future sudden crisis when the king, after a long absence, returns. What a noisy day that is going to be! People who like their religion nice and quiet, dignified and all beautifully controlled, had better keep away that day. The noisiest verse in the Bible is 1 Thessalonians 4:16. There is an archangel shouting his head off; there are trumpets blowing. It is loud enough to wake the dead, I tell you. That will be the biggest meeting of Christians there has ever been. In fact, it will be so big that there is not a stadium on earth that would hold it, so it will be held in the air. You will then see a sudden transformation. You will see how many actually belong to the kingdom, gathered together in one place, and it will include the dead as well. The whole church together for the first time – can you imagine it? It blows my mind.

It will include the people of Israel that day – people who many Christians have written off and said, "Well you've had your chance, now we've got it." Don't you ever get like that. Pride will go before a fall. You read Romans 9–11 carefully. Romans 9 talks about the sovereignty of God choosing Israel, choosing a remnant to be his, and chapter 10 talks about Israel's responsibility and holding them responsible for rejecting the kingdom. There is no incompatibility between divine sovereignty and human responsibility. Again, it is both. Romans 9 is the most marvellous chapter about God's sovereignty that you will read in the New Testament – the potter with the clay, hardening those whom he hardens and having mercy on those on whom he has mercy. But the very next chapter, to keep the picture right, says the Jews are responsible for rejecting. They were not pawns, they were responsible human beings who said no. They did hear the gospel and they turned a deaf ear to it. But if we ask which will win in the end, divine sovereignty or human freewill, chapter 11 tells us that God's freewill will win. I like that, don't you? I believe in divine freewill and it is a bit stronger than human freewill.

God, in his great mercy, has hardened the Jews for a time and passed the kingdom to the Gentiles, but when the full number of the Gentiles is in, God in his mercy is going to soften the Jews again and say: I want you in, too. So all Israel will be saved. Oh, the mercy of God; he never goes back on a promise he has made, and he made promises to those people, which he will never break. They are enemies of the gospel, but for the patriarchs' sake, they are beloved by God. When he loves someone, he does not let them go that easily. So, on that day, all the Gentiles from around the world who have become subjects of the kingdom will be gathered, and the Jewish nation will be gathered also. Jesus, King of kings and Lord of lords, will take over world government.

I believe there will be a millennium. There has to be a time when he reigns on earth. He has got to demonstrate, on earth, that he is King. The thousand years is a literal thousand years or a metaphorical figure for a period of time – I really don't care which – the important thing is that our Jesus will be King over the whole earth and demonstrate what it is like to have such a King – perfect sovereign – and it will mean total disarmament. There will be no more need for any weapons. Can you imagine it? People are so earth-bound that if you talk to them about a heaven, they are not interested, but tell them you know how total nuclear disarmament will come about and they might listen. Tell them you know it is coming and you know the person who is going to be able to bring it. You know the one who is going to take over world government.

We must return briefly to another thing. You may remember I mentioned that the kingdom of God will grow – and the kingdom of Satan. They will both reach a climax. The kingdom of Satan will reach its climax just before the climax of the kingdom of God, and I am referring to the Antichrist. Satan will produce his candidate to be king over the whole earth first. That will be the final, bloody confrontation between the two kingdoms, but God has told us that in his sovereignty he will keep the period of that evil man's power very short for the sake of the elect. So that even when you see Antichrist, you know that God is in total control and has said that he can have the power for just a few years and then God's kingdom takes over. Psalm 2:1–6 helps us to understand:

Why do the nations rage and the peoples plot in vain?
The kings of the earth take their stand
and the rulers gather together
against the Lord and against his anointed one.
'Let us break their chains,' they say,
and throw off their fetters.'
The one enthroned in heaven laughs;
the Lord scoffs at them.
Then he rebukes them in his anger
and terrifies them in his wrath, saying,
'I have installed my king on Zion, my holy hill.'

Lightning Source UK Ltd.
Milton Keynes UK
UKOW06f2350180216

268709UK00014B/452/P